The art of
layered cooking

LASAGNA

Dwayne Ridgaway

LAUREL
GLEN

San Diego, California

Laurel Glen Publishing
An imprint of the Advantage Publishers Group
5880 Oberlin Drive, San Diego, CA 92121-4794
www.laurelglenbooks.com

All notations of errors or omissions should be addressed to Laurel Glen Publishing, Editorial Department, at the above address. All other correspondence (author inquiries, permissions, and rights) concerning the content of this book should be addressed to: Packaged Goods, 33 Commercial Street, Gloucester, MA 01930.

Photography by Ron Manville, with the exception of: Michael Paul Photography: page 116

ISBN 1-59223-155-1

Library of Congress Cataloging-in-Publication Data available upon request.

1 2 3 4 5 07 06 05 04 03

Printed in China.

Editorial Director:
Donna Raskin

Creative and Photo Direction:
Silke Braun

Art Direction:
Claire MacMaster

Managing Editor:
Wendy Simard

Photo Editor:
Jennifer Beal

Design:
Wilson Harvey, London

Photography:
Ron Manville

Food styling:
Tim and Elizabeth Prescott

For my mother and grandmothers, for without them and the
love that their kitchens exude, this book would not be a reality.

Contents

Layer upon Layer
of History

Lasagna belongs to a family of baked pasta dishes known in Italy as *pasticci,* or twice-cooked pasta. For pasticci, the pasta is boiled, mixed, or layered with prepared ingredients or sauces, then baked.

Almost any noodle can be used for pasticci, but lasagna is most likely the original noodle used for baked dishes. For that matter, lasagna is probably the oldest type of pasta, period. It's certainly the easiest to make. After rolling out pasta dough, you're left with a flat, wide noodle—the dictionary definition of "lasagna." But the meaning of lasagna goes deeper than that. Of course, the term "lasagna" refers to the popular casserole that features the noodle. But even deeper, many word historians believe that "lasagna" originally referred to the cooking vessel itself.

Given this word's etymology, it makes sense that "lasagna" now refers to both the noodles and the dish. Sometimes the definition gets stretched even further to include any baked casserole that is layered in a manner similar to traditional lasagna. For instance, some versions of zucchini lasagna layer wide strips of zucchini among sauces and cheeses, omitting the pasta altogether. I've even read a book on "lasagna gardening," an agricultural method that relies on the principle of layering inherent in the classic Italian dish. This makes for three key elements in the definition of lasagna: (1) wide, flat noodles, (2) layers, and (3) a cooking vessel in which the dish is both cooked and served.

In keeping with the more liberal definition of lasagna, the recipes in this book employ at least two, if not all three, of lasagna's key elements. For example, I've included a few Italian layered desserts such as tiramisu and tortes. These dishes don't feature pasta, but they are layered and served in the pan in which they are prepared. You'll also find a lasagna gratin, which uses lasagna noodles and a lasagna pan but dispenses with the time-consuming layering. A few other dishes, such as fresh apple lasagna and Mexican tortilla lasagna, take creative license with the idea of this classic dish. The rest of the book is devoted to variations on the traditional theme of boiled lasagna noodles layered with various cheeses, sauces, and fillings, then cooked and served in the same pan.

chapter 1

Lasagna-**Making Basics**

Not only does lasagna taste good, people love to cook it because it's fairly easy to create and can last for at least two meals. But just because it's simple doesn't mean it's easy. Knowing what ingredients work best can mean the difference between creating a ho-hum staple and an out-of-this world meal.

[Pasta]

The quickest way to get lasagna to the table is to buy and use convenience products, which means you'll probably buy dried lasagna noodles at the grocery store. The best and most reliable choices for dried noodles are brands imported from Italy, which are almost always made with 100% semolina flour. Some of my favorites are Barilla, De Cecco, Del Verde, and Fini.

You have to cook dried lasagna noodles before assembling them into the finished dish. The noodles come in a few styles; the two most popular are flat with curly edges and ribbed with curly edges. I have tested recipes with both and have found that the flat is the best. The noodles help hold the dish together exceptionally well, and if well oiled, the noodles keep fresh for a day or two after being cooked.

[No-Boil Lasagna Noodles]

No-boil lasagna sheets are a modern convenience that eliminates time, pots, and a small amount of your effort in the kitchen. In terms of quality, no-boil noodles should be made of only 100% semolina and water, just like dried lasagna noodles.

The trick to achieving success with no-boil lasagna noodles is in the sauce, or, I should say, in the amount of sauce you use in the dish. These noodles tend to absorb extra moisture from the sauce during the baking process. This creates a dish that's dry, rather than luscious, as the sauce thins down to its heaviest ingredients.

I created the dishes in this book with fresh or dried pasta, but if you want to use no-boil lasagna noodles, simply increase the moisture in the sauces to allow for some absorption. I have found that Del Verde and Barilla offer the two best no-boil choices.

Del Verde goes as far as providing an 8 × 8-inch aluminum baking pan in which to bake your dish. Now, that's convenience.

But here's a little secret: You can actually boil no-boil pasta noodles if you want to. The Barilla no-boil noodles have a nice shape—they are flat with straight edges, which makes them an elegant alternative to curly edged noodles. Also, they are smaller in size, so you can create smaller lasagnas. The flat shape allows them to be boiled and cut to fit any pan, which is very convenient if you want to cook for just one or two people.

[Canned Plum Tomatoes]
I find the canned tomato section of supermarkets to be very overwhelming. Generally speaking, most of the options are good-quality products. I have found, though, that for true freshness, the Italian imported labels are the way to go. And if you really want the best-tasting, truly trustworthy products, find an Italian market where the staff actually knows its products. Frankly, I prefer using simple plum tomatoes when making sauce. I usually don't rely on the other ingredients and herbs that some producers add to their tomatoes.

[Olive Oil]
Like wine, olive oil relies on the climate, soil, and geography in which it's grown to create its most alluring flavor. Traveling through Italy is a journey through many subclimates, and each location produces its own distinctive style of oil.

Tuscan oils are typically pungent and full-bodied, with a fruity appeal. The Chianti region produces oils of noted peppery flavors. Umbrian oils are creamy, with a fruity taste, and Ligurian oils provide sweet and delicate flavors. Choosing an oil is mostly a matter of taste, and, frankly, it's kind of fun to buy a few bottles, pour some samples into saucers, and get some great Italian bread to dip into each kind. You'll probably find a favorite, and when doing your sampling, be sure to drink lots of wine. You'll be bringing the delicious flavors of Italy right into your home.

Whichever type of oil you prefer, and no matter where it is produced, the finest olive oils are those labeled extra-virgin. Extra-virgin means that the oil was mechanically pressed from premium, top-grade olives without the use of heat or chemicals.

Oils simply labeled "olive oil" have been extracted from the olive using heat or chemicals, then filtered and blended to eliminate much of the olives'

flavor. These oils are intended for general cooking purposes where the flavor of the olives isn't that important to the dish. To keep its flavor fresh, store olive oil in dark glass bottles or cans, away from heat and light.

Throughout this book, olive oil is used in many applications. From coating vegetables for grilling to sautéing meats, it is an essential ingredient used for its intense flavors, as in Basic Basil Pesto and Quick Tomato Sauces. Because the need for it varies, I have specified in recipes where you'll need to use extra-virgin oil. While this type of oil can be expensive, it is truly essential to some dishes.

[Sauces]
Sauces are integral to any lasagna. Not only do they lend a layer of texture and flavor to a dish, but they also add moisture for the pasta noodles. In this book, I have identified four sauces basic to Italian cooking, as well as traditional and classic lasagna dishes.

There are as many schools of thought about and "family" traditions for making sauces as there are regions in Italy. While I have made every effort to provide you with traditional, classical sauce recipes, I have also given my own flair to them as well.

For example, many Italian kitchens suggest that there is

no other way to make tomato sauce than to begin with fresh, ripe tomatoes. Now, I truly believe that the flavors of fresh tomatoes are tremendous—in the interest of time, however, there are so many canned tomato products available today that it doesn't make sense to labor so hard to achieve a similar result. The recipe for Quick Tomato Sauce is packed with the fresh flavors of tomato and sweet basil. I use canned whole, peeled plum tomatoes, crushing them during cooking to extract the most flavor. I have found that the whole, peeled tomatoes go through far less processing than diced and crushed ones, so the freshness that I desire is still intact.

You will find that my Quick Tomato Sauce is exactly that— few ingredients and a quick cooking time allow for a flavorful, intense sauce that is readily available.

[Pesto]
I researched pesto extensively to find what I believed to be the undisputed classical method of preparation. Truly classical pesto should be made in a mortar and pestle, crushing basil leaves— devoid of stems—with salt and garlic to achieve a finely minced, vibrant green paste. Then adding fine cheese, olive oil, and pine nuts crushed to a thick consistency. Again, in the

interest of time and to save on unneeded kitchen equipment costs, I use the modern convenience of the food processor. For my pesto, the intense flavor of the best-quality extra-virgin olive oil is paramount to the flavor. The sauce begins in the food processor and is finished by mixing in the cheese by hand. A small amount of butter finalizes the sauce with a rich, velvety sheen.

[Pasta Machines]

Pasta-rolling machines can be found in most department stores and specialty kitchen stores everywhere. It is not necessary to have a rolling machine to make fresh lasagna noodles; however, if you are not comfortable with your accuracy with a rolling pin, then a pasta machine will take away the guesswork. With adjustable thickness gauges, the machine will allow you to gradually roll your dough to the desired thickness by simply adjusting the roller thickness. There are also power motors available as an accessory to make it easier to make fresh pasta sheets.

[Choosing a Baking Dish]

If there is a standard lasagna-baking dish, it would have to be a glass 13 × 9-inch pan. This size is identified as standard because the traditional store-bought, dried lasagna noodles fit the 13 × 9-inch dish perfectly. The next most popular are the 8 × 8-inch dishes—the size of your dish can generally be chosen in regard to how many servings you wish to have. In this book, I have chosen to bake in both sizes of dishes to give you the opportunity to use both.

Choosing a dish for baking your lasagna has generally been left up to personal preference. Dishes can vary in material from clear glass (Pyrex) to colored ceramic, cast iron, and aluminum. There is not much difference to cooking in glass versus ceramic or aluminum. What you want to consider is the immediate use of the dish. Will the lasagna be served immediately or will there be a period of storage? Is the lasagna for family consumption or will it be traveling to another location to be enjoyed by others? The answers to these questions will guide you in choosing the correct baking dish. Baking in disposable aluminum foil gives you the flexibility to either serve the dish immediately, refrigerate it for later, or freeze it for future use. You may even want to consider using a disposable pan if you are sharing your lasagna with a neighbor or taking it to a party.

The comparison of glass to ceramic indicates no differences other than seeing the sides and layers of the dish, which are visible in a glass pan. I have not found any difference in baking times or the texture of the end result when comparing them.

One type of baking dish that some may never consider is cast iron. Cast-iron baking dishes, more prevalent in Southern homes, can be very handy. The baking times will not change, but the end result will tend to be richer, with a crisp crust forming around the edges. In this book, I chose to bake the Mexican Lasagna in a round cast-iron skillet not only because the round tortillas fit well within the skillet, but also because of the cooking characteristics the skillet offers. Cast iron imparts to every dish the flavors of previous dishes, because of what is referred to as "seasoning." A well-seasoned pan will not stick and will bake very evenly. Although it's not a common type of baking dish, there are certainly some great advantages to cooking in cast iron.

[Assembling Lasagna]

Lasagna is basically the art of preparing and layering complementary flavors and textures in a casserole fashion, allowing for the flavors to "bake" together, resulting in rich layers of married intensities. Generally, all lasagnas should begin with lasagna noodles on the bottom to create a support, and end with a layer of sauce and cheeses to create a bubbling, golden top. Everything in between is up to the individual preparing it. Just keep in mind that the lasagna noodles are what bind the dish together. If adequate layers of pasta are used in proportion to the other ingredients, the casserole will maintain its layered configuration when served.

[Storage and Reheating]

Like wine, lasagna improves with age. It's almost as if the word "lasagna" translates to "better the second day." Almost every recipe in this book will improve with overnight refrigeration. This is due in part to a marinating effect. The sauces, pasta, and other ingredients have the opportunity to combine and absorb each other's flavors. Many lasagna dishes can be made in advance, covered, and refrigerated overnight. One advantage to this is that you can prepare a few dishes over the weekend, then pull them out during the week, heat them covered at 400°F for about 20 minutes, and serve.

If you want to freeze lasagna before cooking it, simply cover it tightly with plastic wrap and foil. Label it, date it, and place it in the freezer. When you are ready to serve it, thaw the lasagna in the refrigerator, then bake it as if it were fresh according to the recipe. Lasagna should last about three months in the freezer, provided that its container has an airtight seal. Use aluminum baking dishes when freezing lasagna.

When you are freezing previously baked lasagna, I suggest cutting it into individual portions and wrapping them in plastic wrap and foil, then labeling and dating them before putting them in the freezer. This allows for small amounts to be reheated at a time. Be sure to allow baked lasagna to cool completely before cutting it to freeze in portions. It is best to cool it covered in the refrigerator. This will firm up the dish so that when you cut it, it will maintain its layered square shape. Individual portions of frozen lasagna should last up to three months in the freezer.

If the frozen lasagna seems a bit dry after thawing and baking, heat up some sauce and serve it alongside.

[chapter 2]

Classic Lasagna

Here, feather-light lasagna noodles surround rich layers of hearty meat sauce and creamy béchamel, giving way to timeless tradition. Typically, Lasagna Bolognese would be made with homemade "green" or spinach pasta sheets. Either fresh or store-bought pasta can be used here. If you have the time and the inclination, I strongly urge you to make the green pasta sheets found on page 122 for a truly classic dish.

[serves 9]

Lasagna **Bolognese**

Preheat oven to 350°F. In an oiled 13 × 9-inch baking dish, place a layer of drained noodles, just barely overlapping. Cover with about one third of the meat sauce and then one third of the Béchamel Sauce. Top with about one quarter of the Fontina cheese strips. Repeat layers two more times. Top with a layer of noodles and the remaining cheese strips. Bake uncovered for 45 minutes or until top is golden and bubbly. Remove from oven and let stand for a few minutes before cutting into squares to serve.

1 pound cooked fresh pasta or 1 pound packaged dry pasta cooked according to package instructions

4 cups Bolognese Meat Sauce (page 113)

2 cups Béchamel Sauce (page 113) made with 1/2 peeled onion studded with 2 cloves

1/2 pound Italian Fontina cheese cut into strips

1½ pounds lean ground beef

1 onion, chopped

2 stalks celery, chopped

½ red pepper, chopped

2 cloves garlic, minced

1 tablespoon chopped fresh basil

1 teaspoon dried oregano

1 teaspoon dried thyme

1½ teaspoons salt

1 (29-ounce) can diced tomatoes in juice

2 (6-ounce) cans tomato paste

12 dry lasagna noodles

2 eggs, beaten

2 cups part-skim ricotta cheese

½ cup grated Parmesan cheese

2 tablespoons dried parsley

1 teaspoon salt

1 pound shredded mozzarella cheese

4 tablespoons grated Parmesan cheese

In a skillet over medium heat, brown ground beef, onion, celery, red pepper, and garlic; drain the fat. Mix in basil, oregano, thyme, 1½ teaspoons salt, diced tomatoes, and tomato paste. Simmer for 30 to 45 minutes, stirring occasionally.

Preheat oven to 375°F. Bring a large pot of lightly salted water to a boil. Add lasagna noodles, and cook for 9 minutes, or until al dente; drain. Lay noodles flat on towels and blot dry.

In a medium bowl, mix together the eggs, ricotta, 2 tablespoons Parmesan cheese, parsley, and 1 teaspoon salt.

Oil the bottom and sides of a 9 × 13-inch baking dish. Layer one third of the lasagna noodles in the bottom of the baking dish. Cover the noodles with half of the ricotta mixture, half of the mozzarella cheese, and one third of the sauce. Repeat. Top with remaining noodles and sauce. Sprinkle the remaining Parmesan cheese over the top.

Bake in the preheated oven for 30 minutes. Let stand 10 minutes before serving.

[serves 8]

Classic Italian-American Lasagna

When I was growing up, this dish made its way to our dinner table more times than I can even remember. In my house, however, cottage cheese replaced the ricotta cheese (which you can also do, if you want).

12 dried lasagna noodles

FOR MEATBALLS:

2 pounds ground beef

2 cloves fresh garlic, minced

1/4 cup seasoned bread crumbs

1/4 cup grated Romano cheese

2 eggs

1/2 teaspoon salt

1/2 teaspoon coarse ground black pepper

FOR TOMATO SAUCE:

2 (28-ounce) cans whole peeled plum tomatoes

1 cup fresh basil

1/2 cup tomato sauce

2 tablespoons seasoning salt

1 (6-ounce) can tomato paste with garlic

1/4 teaspoon coarse ground black pepper

FOR CHEESE FILLING:

2 pounds ricotta cheese

3/4 cup Romano cheese

[serves 8]

Mama Rose's Meatball Lasagna

I think the only lasagna recipe that is more traditional than this is Lasagna Bolognese. Meatball Lasagna has been around for years. To find the perfect recipe, I relied on a well-versed Italian to lead me in the right direction. Rose's lasagna recipe has been around for years.

Preheat oven to 400°F. Evenly coat a 9 × 13-inch baking dish with cooking spray or olive oil. In a large pot of boiling, salted water, cook the lasagna noodles to al dente for 10 minutes. Drain the noodles and return them to the pot. Fill the pot with cold water and leave noodles until you're ready to use them. Once ready for assembly, remove one noodle at a time, pat it dry, and place it in the baking dish.

[For meatballs]

In a large mixing bowl, combine all of the ingredients. Using your hands, crush the ingredients together to form a smooth consistency. If needed, add cold water to achieve a moist, yet firm consistency. To form the meatballs, moisten your hands with cold water and roll mounds of the mixture (the size of golf balls) together to form balls. Moisten your hands with cold tap water between each meatball to prevent sticking. Place the meatballs on a platter and set aside.

[For tomato sauce]

Combine all ingredients in a medium stockpot. Bring to a boil, stirring to incorporate, reduce heat to a simmer, and allow to simmer while finishing meatball preparation.

Fill a large skillet with vegetable or canola oil two inches up the sides. Heat on medium to high heat. Once oil is hot, fry the meatballs until brown on all sides, about 5 minutes. Remove the meatballs from the oil and place on a paper towel to drain for a minute or two. Add meatballs to tomato sauce and let it cook for 5 minutes.

[For cheese filling]

In a medium mixing bowl, combine cheeses, stirring thoroughly to combine to a creamy consistency.

[To assemble]

Remove the meatballs from the tomato sauce and place in a mixing bowl. Using a fork or potato masher, crush the meatballs into a crumbly consistency and set aside. In your baking dish, begin with 1 cup of tomato sauce, layer four lasagna noodles, overlapping each other, over the sauce. Top the noodles with the meatball mixture, then add 1 cup of tomato sauce. Top with four more lasagna noodles overlapping each other, then add the ricotta cheese mixture. Layer the remaining lasagna noodles, making sure that they overlap each other. Top with the remaining sauce. Cover the lasagna with aluminum foil and bake for 30 minutes until bubbling. Remove from the oven and let rest for 10 minutes before serving.

1 pound ground beef

4 cups tomato basil sauce

4 cups ricotta cheese

2 cups shredded mozzarella cheese, divided

1 cup grated Parmesan cheese

2 eggs

1 tablespoon fresh parsley, chopped

1 teaspoon salt

1/4 teaspoon ground black pepper

12 no-boil lasagna noodles

[serves 8 to 10]

Easiest-Ever Lasagna

No-boil noodles make this version a cinch to make. Lay them crosswise in the pan and leave ample space around each one; they will expand as they soak up liquid in the oven. When assembling, completely douse the noodles with sauce or cheese so that they cook properly.

In a large skillet, cook the meat, breaking it up with a spoon until browned, about 5 minutes. Drain off excess fat. Stir in the sauce and simmer over medium heat for 10 minutes.

Preheat oven to 350°F. In a large bowl, mix the ricotta, 1 cup of the mozzarella, 3/4 cup of the Parmesan cheese, eggs, parsley, salt, and pepper.

Spoon a layer of the sauce over the bottom of a 9 × 13-inch baking dish. Arrange three noodles crosswise in the pan over the sauce, leaving space around each. Spread one third of the cheese mixture over the noodles. Spoon one quarter of the sauce over the cheese. Repeat the layers of noodles, cheese mixture, and sauce to make a total of four layers of noodles. Top the final layer of noodles with the remaining sauce, 1 cup mozzarella cheese, and 1/4 cup of Parmesan cheese. Cover with foil and bake for 40 minutes. Remove foil and bake until lightly browned, about 10 additional minutes. Let stand 10 minutes before cutting to serve.

2 tablespoons olive oil

2 whole chicken breasts, boned and cut into 1-inch cubes

3 cups sliced mushrooms

2 cloves garlic, minced

1 large onion, chopped

1 teaspoon dried oregano

1 teaspoon dried basil

1 teaspoon dried thyme

1 (28-ounce) can Italian crushed tomatoes with basil

1 (15-ounce) can tomato sauce

3 tablespoons freshly grated Romano cheese plus 1/2 cup

2 cups grated carrot

1/2 teaspoon salt

1 teaspoon coarse ground black pepper

8 ounces lasagna noodles, cooked al dente and drained

6 to 8 slices mozzarella cheese

Preheat oven to 350°F. Evenly coat a 9 × 13-inch baking dish with cooking spray or olive oil. Heat the olive oil in a large skillet over medium to high heat. Add the chicken, mushrooms, garlic, onion, oregano, basil, and thyme. Cook the chicken until it turns white. Stir in the tomatoes, tomato sauce, 3 tablespoons of Romano cheese, carrots, salt, and pepper. Cook uncovered for 5 minutes. To assemble, layer three lasagna noodles in the baking dish, top with half of the chicken mixture, 1/4 cup of Romano cheese, and half of the mozzarella cheese. Layer three more lasagna noodles and top with the remaining chicken mixture, Romano cheese, and mozzarella cheese. Cover and bake for 20 minutes. Remove the cover and continue to bake for 10 minutes or until it is bubbly and the cheese is melted. Remove from oven and let rest for 10 minutes before cutting to serve.

[serves 8]

Chicken Lasagna with Mushrooms and Herbs

When I began telling people about this cookbook, the recipes began to pour in. Well, needless to say, they didn't all make the cut, but one that did is this easy, very flavorful chicken dish from my friend Jen.

Zucchini have such a fresh, crisp flavor that it was only natural to incorporate them into a lasagna dish. With this dish, I have breaded and fried the zucchini to intensify their flavors.

[serves 8]

Fried Zucchini Lasagna with Spicy Tomato Sauce

Preheat oven to 400°F. Coat a 9 × 13-inch baking dish with cooking spray or olive oil. In a large pot of boiling, salted water, cook the pasta noodles until al dente, about 10 minutes. Drain and rinse under cold water and lay on a towel to dry.

In a medium bowl, combine flour, bread crumbs, salt, black pepper, and paprika. In a small bowl, combine milk and beaten eggs. Dredge each zucchini slice in flour, then in milk mixture, then back in flour. Add vegetable oil to a skillet and fry zucchini over medium to high heat for about 4 minutes until golden brown. Remove zucchini from oil and drain on paper towels.

[For the mushroom filling]
Using a large skillet, over medium to high heat, melt butter and oil. Sauté onions

12 lasagna noodles	**FOR FRIED ZUCCHINI:**	**FOR MUSHROOM FILLING:**	**FOR CHEESE FILLING:**
4 cups Slow-Simmered Tomato Sauce (page 120) or Quick Tomato Sauce (page 117)	1 cup flour	2 tablespoons unsalted butter	1 (24-ounce) container cottage cheese
2 tomatoes, sliced thin	1/3 cup seasoned bread crumbs	1 tablespoon extra-virgin olive oil	1/2 cup mascarpone cheese
	1 teaspoon salt	2 medium onions, thinly sliced	2 cups Parmigiano-Reggiano cheese, divided
	1 teaspoon coarse ground black pepper	3 cloves garlic, minced	1/4 cup minced fresh basil
	1 teaspoon paprika	15 ounces sliced mushrooms	1/2 teaspoon salt
	1 cup milk	1/2 teaspoon salt	1/4 teaspoon coarse ground black pepper
	2 eggs, beaten	1/2 teaspoon coarse ground black pepper	
	4 cups vegetable oil	1 tablespoon sesame seeds	
	2 pounds zucchini, thinly sliced	1/2 teaspoon dried thyme	

and garlic until translucent, add mushrooms, salt, pepper, sesame seeds, and thyme, and continue cooking for about 10 minutes until mushrooms are browned.

[For the cheese filling]
In a medium-sized mixing bowl, combine the cottage cheese, mascarpone, 1 cup of the Parmigiano-Reggiano, basil, salt, and pepper. Stir well.

[To assemble]
Place $1^1/_2$ cups of sauce in the bottom of the baking dish. Top with three lasagna noodles, then with half the fried zucchini, half the mushroom mixture, then a layer of the sliced tomatoes. Sprinkle with $^1/_2$ cup Parmigiano-Reggiano, then top with $1^1/_2$ cups more sauce. Layer with three additional noodles, then with three quarters of the cheese filling. Top with three more noodles, the remaining sauce, the remaining mushroom filling, then a layer of fried zucchini and the remaining cheese. Sprinkle with a dusting of Parmigiano-Reggiano. Bake, uncovered, for 30 minutes or until the top layer of cheese is golden brown and the sides are bubbly. Remove from oven and let rest for 10 minutes before cutting to serve.

Polenta is such a versatile food. In this recipe I have prepared it to a rich, creamy texture, flavored it with Parmesan cheese, and allowed it to cool for use in place of lasagna noodles. The polenta layers, the robust flavor of linguica, and the delicate nature of the Swiss chard go well together.

[serves 8]

Polenta Lasagna **with Linguica and Swiss Chard**

FOR POLENTA:

2 cups milk

1 tablespoon unsalted butter

1/2 teaspoon salt

1 teaspoon sugar

1 cup stone-ground yellow cornmeal or fine yellow grits

1/4 cup grated Parmesan cheese

FOR THE FILLING:

4 tablespoons unsalted butter

4 tablespoons olive oil

1 medium yellow onion, finely chopped

1 carrot, peeled and finely chopped

1 celery stalk, finely chopped

2 cloves garlic, chopped

1/2 pound linguica or chorizo chopped to 1/4-inch dice

1/2 cup dry red wine

1 (14-ounce) can diced tomatoes with purée

1/4 teaspoon red pepper flakes

salt and freshly cracked black pepper

FOR SWISS CHARD PURÉE:

1 bunch (about 1 pound) Swiss chard, washed, patted dry, and roughly chopped

1/2 cup crumbled feta cheese

1/2 teaspoon freshly ground nutmeg

1/4 teaspoon ground ginger

2 cloves garlic, minced

3 tablespoons fresh basil, minced

1 teaspoon fresh Italian parsley, minced

1/2 cup heavy cream

1/2 pound fresh mozzarella cheese, sliced

[For polenta]

Combine milk, butter, salt, and sugar in a heavy-bottomed saucepan (a Teflon-coated one works best). Bring to a simmer, just until steaming. Add cornmeal in a steady stream, whisking continuously to combine it and prevent lumps from forming. Once combined, reduce the heat to a simmer and continue to cook, stirring continuously, until the mixture is thick and begins to pull away from the sides of the pot, about 2 to 5 minutes. Remove from the heat and add the Parmesan cheese. Combine thoroughly.

Oil a 10 × 15-inch sheet pan. Pour the polenta into the prepared pan, spreading it flat with an oiled spatula. Cool until firm, about 1 hour. (The polenta can be made up to a day ahead. Cover the pan with plastic wrap and refrigerate it.)

[For sausage filling]

In a large saucepan over medium heat, melt 2 tablespoons of butter with 2 tablespoons of olive oil. Add the onion, carrot, and celery, and cook, stirring, until tender but not browned, about 10 minutes. Stir in the garlic. Add the sausage and cook, stirring, until browned, about 10 minutes. Add the wine and cook until the liquid evaporates, about 2 additional minutes. Add the tomatoes and their juice, the parsley, and the red pepper flakes. Stir to combine. Season with salt and pepper, and reduce the heat to a simmer. Simmer uncovered until the mixture is thickened, about 30 minutes.

[For Swiss chard purée]

In a medium saucepan, heat the remaining 2 tablespoons of butter with the remaining 2 tablespoons of olive oil. Add the Swiss chard, tossing it to coat it with oil. Cover and let steam until the chard is tender and bright green in color, about 5 minutes. Stir occasionally to ensure that the chard is tender. Remove the saucepan from the heat and set it aside. Preheat the oven to 400°F. Oil a 9 × 13-inch baking dish. In a food processor, combine the chard, feta cheese, nutmeg, ginger, garlic, basil, and parsley. Process the mixture until puréed. Add the cream, scrape down the sides, and process the mixture until it is well combined and creamy.

[To assemble]

Remove the polenta from the refrigerator. Cut the polenta into twelve equal squares. Arrange half of the squares in the bottom of the baking dish. Spoon on half of the Swiss chard purée, coating the polenta evenly. Top the purée with half of the sausage mixture. Top the sausage with half of the fresh mozzarella cheese slices. Repeat the layers using the remaining ingredients. Bake until the cheese melts and the sauce is bubbling, about 30 minutes. Let stand for 5 minutes before serving. Serve hot, directly from the oven.

2 tablespoons vegetable or olive oil

1 (16-ounce) package dry lasagna noodles or 1 pound fresh noodles

2 cups Slow-Simmered Tomato Sauce (page 120), Quick Tomato Sauce (page 117), or 1 (26-ounce) spaghetti sauce

2 pounds ricotta or cottage cheese

1/2 cup chopped fresh basil

1/2 cup chopped fresh parsley

8 ounces shredded mozzarella cheese

8 ounces crumbled feta cheese

1 cup grated Parmesan cheese

[serves 9]

Four-Cheese Lasagna

Let the combination of cheeses in this dish do all the work. The most difficult part of this dish is selecting a sauce. The Slow-Simmered Tomato Sauce will give it a deep, rich flavor whereas the Quick Tomato Sauce will impart a more fresh, spring taste. Whatever your decision, the cheeses will pair perfectly and the flavors will be simple but elegant.

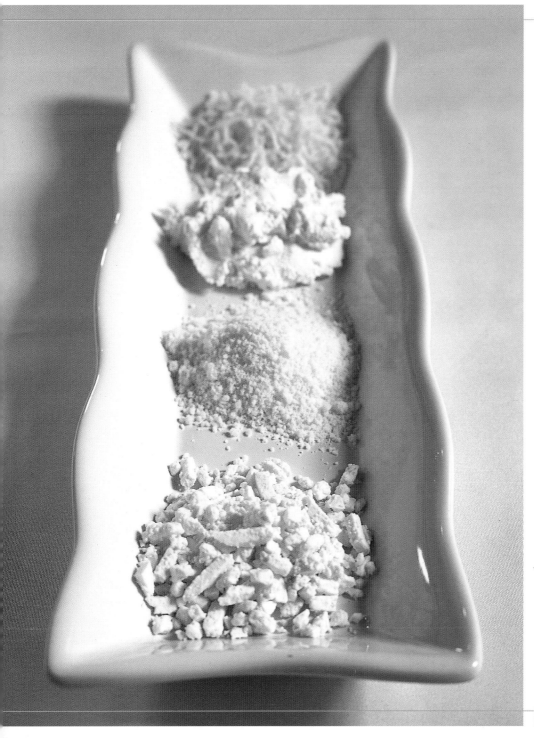

Preheat oven to 375°F. Oil the sides and bottom of a 9 × 13-inch baking dish. Bring a large pot of lightly salted water to a boil. Add dried pasta and cook for 8 to 10 minutes, or until al dente. If using fresh pasta, cook for only 2 to 4 minutes.

In a blender or with an electric mixer, blend the tomato sauce and ricotta cheese together until smooth. In a small bowl, combine the basil and parsley. Spoon a little of the sauce mixture into the bottom of the baking dish. Place a layer of cooked noodles over the sauce, and sprinkle a portion of the mozzarella, feta, Parmesan, and herbs over the noodles. Repeat the layering of sauce, noodles, cheeses, and herbs, finishing with a cheese layer sprinkled with remaining herbs.

Bake in the preheated oven for 30 to 45 minutes until the cheese is bubbly and golden. Remove from the oven and let rest for 10 minutes before slicing to serve.

12 sheets dry lasagna noodles

1 cup ricotta cheese

4 ounces goat cheese

8 ounces Fontina cheese, shredded

8 ounces mozzarella cheese, shredded

1 recipe Basic Basil Pesto (page 118)

6 ounces roasted red peppers, drained and thinly sliced

6 ounces roasted yellow peppers, drained and thinly sliced

[serves 4 to 6]

Pesto Lasagna with Roasted Red and Yellow Peppers

This is a great take on the traditional Lasagna con Pesto from the Ligurian region of Italy. A bright summer day and a silky glass of Pinot Grigio are the best accompaniments for this dish.

Preheat oven to 375°F.

Oil bottom and sides of an 8 × 8-inch baking dish. Bring a large pot of salted water to a boil. Boil pasta noodles for 10 minutes until al dente.

In a small bowl, combine the ricotta and goat cheeses, and blend well. In another small bowl, combine the Fontina and mozzarella cheeses. Line the bottom of the baking dish with three sheets of pasta, and top with one third of the pesto topping and one third of the Fontina cheese mixture. Add another layer of three pasta sheets.

Top with half of the ricotta cheese mixture and then with two thirds of the roasted red and yellow peppers, followed by one third of the Fontina cheese mixture. Then add three more sheets of pasta. Repeat with a layer of pesto, then the remaining Fontina cheese mixture, three pasta sheets, ricotta cheese mixture, roasted peppers, and the pesto as the last layer.

Bake for 30 minutes until it is bubbly and the pesto begins to darken around the edges. Remove from oven and let rest 10 minutes before cutting to serve. For an easier, thinner dish, omit the ricotta cheese mixture from the layers. The result is less rich and a bit oilier, but still tastes terrific.

Cook lasagna noodles according to package directions. Drain them and lay them flat on a towel to dry. In a large skillet over medium heat, sauté the onion, mushrooms, and garlic in oil until they are tender and the mushrooms begin to give off their juices and darken. Place the onion and mushroom mixture in a mixing bowl and add the cream cheese. Gradually stir in the cottage cheese, mozzarella cheese, egg, basil, salt, and pepper. Chop the shrimp and crab and add to the mixture; combine well. In another mixing bowl, combine the mushroom soup, milk, and wine. Oil a 9 × 13-inch baking dish and coat the bottom with half of the mushroom mixture. To assemble roulades, lay the lasagna noodles flat on a large work surface, and spread the seafood mixture evenly over the lasagna noodles, staying close to the edge of the pasta. Begin at one end and roll the noodle up into a cylinder. Place it seam-side down in the baking dish. Repeat with remainder of the noodles and filling. Top roulades with remainder of mushroom sauce, and top with Parmesan cheese. Bake for 20 to 30 minutes until the tops are bubbling and begin to brown. Remove roulades from oven and let them rest for 5 minutes before serving. Serve two roulades per person, garnishing them with fresh basil leaves and sauce from the bottom of the baking dish.

[serves 6]

Seafood Lasagna **Roulades**

This is a tremendous dish with intense flavors and a very elegant presentation. The roulades are such a simple way to use lasagna noodles, with such beautiful results. Serve these with fresh steamed or roasted asparagus spears. Best of all, they are so easy to prepare, taking very little time to pull together for an intimate dinner.

12 lasagna noodles

2 tablespoons olive oil

1 cup onion, chopped

1 cup shiitake mushrooms, rinsed clean and dried, finely chopped

1 clove garlic, finely minced

8 ounces cream cheese

1 1/2 cups cottage cheese

1/2 cup mozzarella cheese, shredded

1 egg

1 tablespoon chopped fresh basil or 2 teaspoons dried

salt and pepper

1 pound boiled baby shrimp

7 ounces crabmeat, cleaned

2 cups condensed mushroom soup

1/3 cup milk

1/3 cup dry white wine

1/4 cup grated Parmesan cheese

Fresh basil leaves for garnish

1 pound ricotta cheese

3 tablespoons fresh basil, chopped

1 tablespoon dried oregano

2 eggs

1/8 teaspoon red pepper flakes

1/4 cup grated Parmesan cheese

1 pound dried lasagna noodles or fresh pasta sheets cut into lasagna noodles

2 1/4 cups Quick Tomato Sauce (page 117)

1/2 pound prosciutto, thinly sliced

1/2 pound Genoa salami, thinly sliced

1/2 pound smoked deli ham, thinly sliced

1/2 pound sweet capicola, thinly sliced

1/2 pound provolone cheese, thinly sliced

1/2 pound shredded mozzarella cheese

Preheat oven to 375°F. Coat the bottom and sides of a 9 × 13-inch baking dish evenly with olive oil. In a large mixing bowl, combine ricotta cheese, basil, oregano, eggs, pepper flakes, and Parmesan cheese. Mix until eggs are thoroughly combined.

In a large pot of salted, boiling water, cook the dried pasta according to package directions; cook fresh pasta for 2 minutes. Drain the pasta and rinse it with cold water. Place it on a paper towel to dry before using it in the dish.

Place 3/4 cup tomato sauce on the bottom of the baking dish. Top with a layer of lasagna noodles. Top noodles with 1/3 cup of the ricotta cheese mixture, spreading evenly over the noodles. Top with another layer of pasta. Top pasta with half of the meats, layering them evenly. Top the meat with half of the provolone, and top this with half of the shredded mozzarella cheese. Repeat with a layer of pasta, then 3/4 cup of sauce, then 1/3 cup ricotta cheese mixture. Top the ricotta cheese mixture with another layer of pasta, then the remainder of the meats, provolone cheese, and mozzarella cheese. Finish with a final layer of pasta, topped with the remainder of the tomato sauce and the remaining ricotta cheese mixture.

Coat a large sheet of aluminum foil with oil and cover the baking pan with it, oil-side down. Bake for 30 minutes, covered. Remove foil and bake for an additional 15 to 20 minutes or until the top is bubbly and the cheese begins to brown. Remove the lasagna from the oven and let it rest for 10 minutes before cutting to serve.

[serves 9]

Italian Grinder Lasagna

Sitting in a little Italian pizzeria one day, I ordered the meaty stuffed pizza. One bite into it and I thought, "This has to be a lasagna." I love the dense texture of this dish—I believe you will, too.

chapter 3

Lasagna **Around the World**

9 dried lasagna noodles

1 tablespoon butter

2 tablespoons extra-virgin olive oil

1 small onion, chopped

3 cloves garlic, minced

1 small green bell pepper, chopped

1 small red pepper, chopped

1 pound skinless, boneless chicken breasts, cooked and diced

1/2 teaspoon cayenne pepper

2 tablespoons apple cider vinegar

2 tablespoons Worcestershire sauce

1 tablespoon Thai curry paste, optional

4 cups Quick Tomato Sauce (page 117) or Slow-Simmered Tomato Sauce (page 120)

1 1/2 cups water

3 tablespoons hot sauce

1 egg, beaten

1 (15-ounce) container ricotta cheese

2 cups shredded mozzarella cheese

3/4 cup crumbled blue or Gorgonzola cheese

Preheat oven to 350°F. Evenly coat a 9 × 13-inch baking dish with cooking spray or olive oil. In a large pot of boiling, salted water, cook the lasagna noodles until al dente, about 10 minutes. Drain and rinse under cold water, and set aside on a towel to dry.

[For chicken mixture]
In a large skillet over medium to high heat, melt the butter and oil. Sauté the onion, garlic, and peppers until tender and onions become translucent, about 5 minutes. Add chicken and cayenne pepper, stir, and cook for an additional 2 minutes. Add vinegar, Worcestershire sauce, and Thai curry paste, stir, and continue to cook for another minute. Add tomato sauce and water, bring to a boil for 1 minute, add hot sauce, reduce heat, and allow to cook for 10 more minutes. Remove from heat and set aside. In a medium mixing bowl, combine the beaten egg with the ricotta cheese and set aside.

[To assemble]
Layer the bottom of the baking dish with three lasagna noodles, top with 1 1/2 cups of the chicken mixture and half of the ricotta cheese mixture, and sprinkle with half of the mozzarella cheese. Top with three more noodles and repeat with 1 1/2 cups chicken mixture, remaining ricotta cheese, and remaining mozzarella cheese. Top with one last layer of lasagna noodles and remaining chicken mixture. Cover pan and bake for 30 minutes. Remove cover, sprinkle crumbled blue cheese on top, and bake an additional 10 minutes until top is golden and bubbly. Remove from oven and let rest for 10 minutes before cutting to serve.

[serves 8]

Buffalo Chicken Lasagna

A great Super Bowl Sunday dish, without all the napkins. You can eat this buffalo chicken with a fork rather than your hands and still have all the great, spicy flavors of your favorite hot wings. If you want, dip some fresh celery sticks into the sauce.

- 3 pounds of eggplant, peeled, sliced 1/2 inch thick
- 4 tablespoons extra-virgin olive oil
- 2 pounds ground lamb
- 2 tablespoons olive oil, extra
- 2 large yellow onions, chopped
- 1/2 cup shredded carrot
- 1/2 cup chopped leeks
- 3 cloves garlic, finely chopped
- 2 (28-ounce) cans peeled, diced tomatoes
- 2 tablespoons tomato paste
- 1/2 cup red wine
- 1 cup beef stock or broth
- 1 tablespoon dried oregano
- 2 sprigs fresh thyme
- 1 teaspoon paprika
- 2 bay leaves
- 1/2 cup chopped fresh Italian parsley
- 1 teaspoon ground cumin
- 2 teaspoons dried basil
- 1 teaspoon ground cinnamon
- 1 tablespoon chopped fresh mint, optional
- Pinch ground cloves
- Salt and coarse ground black pepper
- 3 cups Béchamel Sauce (page 113)
- 1/4 teaspoon nutmeg
- 1/2 pound feta cheese plus 1/2 cup
- Cream or milk as needed
- 9 lasagna noodles, dried or fresh
- 1/4 cup freshly grated Parmesan cheese
- 1/4 cup fine, dried bread crumbs

[serves 9]

Greek-Style Lamb and Eggplant Lasagna

Sometimes referred to as *moussaka,* rich meat sauce using lamb with herbs and spices is a Greek tradition. Both lamb and eggplant are popular in Greek cuisine, but they are also tremendously appreciated in Italian kitchens.

Preheat oven to 400°F.

[To prepare eggplant]
Peel and cut into slices 1/2 inch thick. Place eggplant slices in a colander, sprinkle them with salt, and let them stand for 1 hour to drain off juices. Rinse the eggplant in cold water and pat dry. Coat both sides of sliced eggplant generously with extra-virgin olive oil. Place the eggplant on a baking sheet in the oven, and bake for 15 to 20 minutes, turning once until both sides are browned. Transfer to a paper towel to drain.

[To prepare meat sauce]
In a large stockpot or saucepan, heat the oil over medium to high heat. Brown the lamb, about 10 minutes, breaking it up into small chunks as it cooks. Add the onions, carrot, and leeks. Cook until tender, about 15 minutes. Add the garlic, tomatoes, and tomato paste. Cook for an additional 2 minutes, stirring to combine. Add the red wine, beef broth, herbs and spices. Reduce the heat and simmer for about 30 minutes. The recipe makes more meat sauce than is necessary for this dish. Serve the extra alongside the lasagna slices.

Meanwhile, in a medium saucepan over medium heat, heat the Béchamel Sauce with the nutmeg and feta cheese. Heat through, melting the feta. Add cream or milk, a little at a time, if the sauce appears to be too thick to pour.

[To assemble]

Coat a 9 × 13-inch baking dish evenly with cooking spray or olive oil. Place three pasta noodles in the bottom, and top with an even layer of half of the eggplant, then about 2 cups of meat sauce and half of the Béchamel Sauce. Sprinkle with Parmesan cheese. Add another layer of pasta sheets, topping with the remainder of the eggplant and 2 cups of meat sauce. Top with the remaining three pasta sheets, then with the remaining Béchamel. Sprinkle the top with bread crumbs and $1/2$ cup crumbled feta cheese. Place in the oven and bake for 30 minutes or until golden and bubbly. Remove from the oven and let rest for 10 minutes before cutting to serve.

2 tablespoons extra-virgin olive oil

1 large onion, minced

3 ounces prosciutto di Parma, finely chopped

1/2 cup Italian parsley, finely chopped

2 tablespoons minced shallots

1 pound assorted wild and exotic mushrooms (oyster, shiitake, lobster, cremini, etc.)

2 cups beef broth

2 tablespoons garlic, minced

3 tablespoons fresh basil, chopped

1 tablespoon fresh oregano, chopped

2/3 cups dry white wine

1 (28-ounce) can plus 1 (14-ounce) can crushed tomatoes in purée

1/4 teaspoon paprika

1/4 teaspoon cayenne pepper

Salt and pepper

2 cups plus 2 tablespoons grated Parmigiano-Reggiano cheese

1 cup grated mozzarella cheese plus 1/4 cup

1/2 cup heavy cream

1/4 cup milk

1 pound dried pasta sheets cooked according to package directions or 1 pound fresh pasta blanched for 2 minutes and drained

Preheat the oven to 350°F. Lightly oil a 9 × 13-inch baking dish.

In a large sauté pan, heat the olive oil. When the oil is hot, sauté the onions and prosciutto for about 3 minutes or until the onions are wilted and begin to caramelize.

Add 1/2 cup of minced parsley, shallots, and mushrooms. Combine and sauté them for about 5 minutes or until the mushrooms begin to brown and soften. Add 2 cups of beef broth, stirring vigorously to deglaze the pan—continue to cook for an additional 45 minutes to concentrate the flavors. Season with salt and pepper. Stir in the garlic, basil, and oregano. Cook for an additional 3 minutes to combine the flavors. Remove the mixture from the heat. Strain the mushroom mixture, reserving the liquid.

Pour the liquid back into the sauté pan. Heat and stir vigorously to remove any particles along the sides of the pan. Add the wine and continue to deglaze the pan. Continue to cook the liquid until a glaze is formed, stirring occasionally. Add the tomatoes, paprika, and cayenne, and combine thoroughly. Continue to cook for 20 minutes, stirring occasionally. Season with salt and pepper. Add the mushroom mixture to the sauce. Combine and remove the sauce from the heat.

[To assemble]
Spoon a small amount of the sauce on the bottom of the baking dish, covering evenly. Layer pasta sheets over the sauce, being careful not to overlap them. Cut the pasta sheets to fit the baking dish if necessary. Repeat with a thick layer of mushroom sauce. Sprinkle with Parmigiano-Reggiano and a generous amount of mozzarella cheese. Top with three additional sheets of pasta and repeat with remaining mushroom sauce, Parmesan cheese, mozzarella cheese, and pasta sheets. Ensure that the last layer in the baking dish is the pasta sheets. Mix 1/2 cup heavy cream with 1/4 cup milk, 2 tablespoons Parmigiano-Reggiano cheese, and 1/4 cup mozzarella cheese. Season with salt and pepper. Pour over the top of the lasagna. Cover the lasagna with foil and bake for 30 minutes. Remove the cover and bake for an additional 15 to 20 minutes or until the top layer of cheese becomes brown and bubbly. Remove from oven. Allow to rest for 10 minutes before cutting to serve. If there is any remaining mushroom sauce, serve alongside the lasagna.

[serves 9]

Robust Tomato and Wild Mushroom Lasagna

Tomatoes and wild mushrooms come together in this hearty, wildly flavorful lasagna. With a bite of cayenne, the mushrooms' exotic tastes offer layers of rich, intense flavors throughout the dish.

Preheat oven to 350°F. Evenly coat the sides and bottom of a 9 × 13-inch baking dish with cooking spray or olive oil. In a large pot of boiling, salted water, cook the pasta until al dente—10 minutes for dry noodles, 2 to 3 minutes for fresh. Remove pasta from hot water and run under cold water. Set aside on a towel to dry.

In a small mixing bowl, combine 3 eggs, garlic powder, onion powder, 1 cup Parmesan cheese, Italian seasoning, cayenne pepper, salt, and black pepper. In a separate shallow dish, combine the flour with the bread crumbs.

Heat oil in a large skillet. Dredge eggplant slices in flour, then in egg mixture, and then in flour again. Fry slices in preheated oil, two to three slices at a time, until browned on both sides, about 2 to 3 minutes per side. Remove slices from oil and place on paper towels to drain. Continue until all slices are fried.

In a large bowl, combine ricotta cheese, 1/2 cup mozzarella cheese, remaining 1 cup Parmesan cheese, parsley, basil, remaining egg, and spinach, and mix well.

[To assemble]
Layer one third of the tomato sauce in the bottom of the baking dish, then three lasagna noodles, half the eggplant slices, half the tomato slices, three additional lasagna noodles, ricotta cheese mixture, three more lasagna noodles, one third of the sauce, remaining eggplant, then repeat with the tomato slices, lasagna noodles, and tomato sauce, and top with remaining 1/2 cup mozzarella cheese. Cover with aluminum foil coated with cooking spray, bake for 20 minutes, remove aluminum foil, and continue to bake for an additional 15 minutes until cheese is browned and bubbly. Remove from oven and let rest for 10 minutes before cutting to serve.

[serves 8]

Eggplant and Tomato
Lasagna **Gratin**

Two Italian staples, eggplant and tomato, blend together to melt into a flavorful dish rich in Italian tradition. This lasagna combines the intensely flavorful breaded and fried eggplant with juicy vine-fresh tomatoes to create a layered gratin.

12 lasagna noodles, dried or fresh

4 eggs

1 tablespoon garlic powder

1 teaspoon onion powder, optional

2 cups grated Parmesan cheese, divided

1 tablespoon Italian seasoning

$1/2$ teaspoon cayenne pepper

$1/2$ teaspoon salt

$1/2$ teaspoon coarse ground black pepper

1 cup flour

$1/4$ cup seasoned bread crumbs

2 cups vegetable oil for frying

2 large eggplants, peeled and cut into $1/4$-inch slices

1 (15-ounce) container ricotta cheese

1 cup shredded mozzarella cheese

2 tablespoons fresh Italian parsley, minced

$1/4$ cup fresh basil, minced

1 (10-ounce) package frozen chopped spinach, thawed, drained, and pressed dry

3 cups Quick Tomato Sauce (page 117) or Slow-Simmered Tomato Sauce (page 120)

4 vine-ripened tomatoes, sliced $1/4$ inch thick, seasoned with salt and black pepper

1 pound chicken breasts, cooked and cut into chunks

2 tablespoons olive oil

1/2 cup chopped onion

1/2 cup chopped red bell pepper

1/2 cup frozen corn kernels, thawed

2 cloves garlic, chopped

1 1/2 teaspoons ground cumin

1 teaspoon chili powder

1 (15-ounce) can black beans, rinsed and drained

1 (16-ounce) can refried black beans

2 cups canned tomato sauce

1/2 cup salsa

1 (10-ounce) can enchilada sauce

1/4 cup chopped fresh cilantro plus 2 tablespoons for garnishing

9 corn tortillas

8 ounces shredded cheddar cheese

6 ounces shredded Monterey Jack cheese

1/4 cup sliced black olives (optional)

1/4 cup sour cream for garnish

8 sprigs fresh cilantro for garnish

[serves 8]

Mexican Black Bean Lasagna

Replacing lasagna noodles with tender corn tortillas gives a Southwestern twist to an Italian classic. The use of black beans keeps down the calories, while fresh vegetables and spices impart great flavors. Olé!

Preheat oven to 350°F. Spray the sides and bottom of a 9 × 13-inch baking dish with nonstick cooking spray. In a medium saucepan, bring an ample amount of water to a boil to cook the chicken. Boil the chicken for about 10 minutes until cooked through.

Remove from water and set aside to cool. Once it is cool to the touch, chop the chicken into small chunks. In a large skillet on medium-high heat, heat the olive oil. Add the onion, pepper, corn, and garlic. Sauté the vegetables until they are wilted and translucent, about 10 minutes. Add the cumin and chili powder. Continue to cook for an additional 2 minutes. Add the black beans and chicken. Stir to incorporate flavors and heat through.

Remove the mixture from the heat and set aside. Place a medium-sized saucepan on medium heat and add the refried beans, tomato sauce, salsa, enchilada sauce, and fresh cilantro. Heat to a boil and remove from the heat.

[To assemble]
Place one third of the tomato sauce mixture on the bottom of the baking dish; cover with three tortillas. Top the tortillas with half of the chicken mixture then another one third of the sauce, topping this with half of the cheddar cheese. Repeat the layers with three tortillas, the remaining chicken mixture, sauce, and cheddar cheese, then top all this with three more tortillas, Monterey Jack cheese, and sliced black olives. Place in the oven uncovered, and bake for 20 to 30 minutes until the top is browned and bubbly. Remove from oven and let rest for 10 minutes before cutting to serve. To serve, place the lasagna on a plate, put a tablespoon of sour cream on top, and garnish with a sprig of cilantro.

Straight from New Orleans, this intensely flavored dish, topped with a unique cornbread crust, is easy to make and delicious. I have combined cayenne pepper, chili paste, and hot pepper sauce with garden-fresh vegetables to create this truly Creole experience. The cornbread topping browns to a dense, moist crust.

[serves 9]

Bourbon Street Lasagna **with Cornbread Crust**

9 sheets fresh or dry lasagna noodles

6 tablespoons vegetable or olive oil

2 stalks celery, chopped

1 green bell pepper, chopped

1 red pepper, chopped

1/2 onion, chopped

1 cup frozen corn kernels, thawed

2 cups fresh okra, sliced

11/2 tablespoons fresh thyme leaves, chopped, or 21/2 teaspoons dried

11/2 tablespoons fresh sage leaves, chopped, or 21/2 teaspoons dried

11/2 tablespoons fresh rosemary, chopped, or 21/2 teaspoons dried

1 to 2 cups water

1 cup chopped boneless, skinless chicken breasts

7 ounces smoked sausage (such as andouille), sliced in fourths, then in chunks

FOR CREOLE SAUCE:

6 tablespoons unsalted butter

1/2 cup all-purpose flour

2 cups chicken or vegetable stock or canned broth

2 cups Quick Tomato Sauce (page 117)

1 teaspoon chili powder

1/2 teaspoon cayenne pepper

1 teaspoon chili paste or Thai curry paste

1 teaspoon coarse ground black pepper

1/2 teaspoon hot sauce

FOR CORNBREAD TOPPING:

1/2 cup coarse yellow cornmeal

11/2 cups all-purpose flour

1/3 cup firmly packed light brown sugar

1 teaspoon baking powder

1/4 teaspoon baking soda

1/2 teaspoon salt

1/2 teaspoon ground coriander

1 large egg, lightly beaten

11/2 cups buttermilk

1/4 cup vegetable oil

FOR ASSEMBLY:

4 ounces shredded mozzarella cheese

4 ounces shredded Monterey Jack cheese

Preheat oven to 375°F. Oil the sides and bottom of a 9 × 13-inch baking dish. In a large stockpot of boiling, salted water, cook the noodles until al dente, about 10 minutes for dry, 2 to 3 minutes for fresh. Drain the pasta, rinse with cold water, and set aside on paper towels to dry.

In a large skillet on medium-high heat, add 4 tablespoons of olive oil. When the oil is hot, add the celery, green pepper, red pepper, and onion. Sauté until translucent and tender, about 5 minutes. Add the corn and continue to cook for an additional 2 minutes, then add the okra. Stir the okra into the mixture and continue to cook. The okra will begin to get gummy and possibly stick to the bottom of the pan. If the skillet appears to be dry and the vegetables are sticking, add 1 cup of water to moisten.

Continue to cook until the okra is tender and bright green in color, about 5 minutes. Add the thyme, sage, and rosemary. At this point, if the mixture appears to be overly dry, again add up to 1 cup of water and cook until a thick liquid forms. Remove the skillet from the heat and set it aside. In a separate medium skillet, heat the remaining 2 tablespoons of olive oil on medium to high heat. Add the chicken and sausage, and cook until browned and cooked through, about 10 minutes. Add the chicken and sausage to the vegetable mixture and combine.

[To prepare the Creole sauce]
In a medium saucepan over medium to high heat, melt the butter and add the flour; using a whisk, stir continuously, cooking the mixture until a rich, dark brown color is achieved, along with a nutty aroma. This is the roux (thickener) for the sauce. Add the chicken stock a little at a time, stirring vigorously after each addition to incorporate the liquid thoroughly and prevent lumps. Be careful of the initial steam that will rise from adding the chicken stock. After all the chicken stock is incorporated, reduce the heat to low and add the tomato sauce; stir and cook for 5 minutes. Add the chili powder, cayenne pepper, chili paste, black pepper, and hot sauce, stir to incorporate, and continue to cook for 5 minutes. Remove the saucepan from the heat and set it aside.

[To prepare cornbread topping]
In a medium-sized mixing bowl, combine all the dry ingredients; using a whisk, stir them until thoroughly mixed. Pushing from the middle of the bowl outward with a spoon, form a well in the center of the dry ingredients. Add the egg, buttermilk, and oil in the well. Working from the sides inward with the whisk, begin to incorporate the dry ingredients gradually, then whisk vigorously to combine the ingredients. The slow incorporation of the wet ingredients into the dry will prevent lumps from forming in the batter. Set aside for assembly.

[To assemble]
In your baking dish, place 1¹/₂ cups of Creole sauce, evenly coating the bottom of the pan; top with three sheets of noodles. Top noodles with half of the vegetable filling, and sprinkle with half of the mozzarella and Monterey Jack cheeses. Repeat the layers with pasta, then 1¹/₂ cups of sauce, pasta again, the remainder of the vegetable filling, and finally the remainder of the cheese. Using your hands, firmly pack the lasagna layers in the pan, making room for the cornbread batter on top. Drizzle the cornbread batter over the top in a solid layer, evenly coating the top layer. You may not need all of the batter; this depends on the thickness of your layers. Place the baking dish on a large cookie sheet to catch any drippings. Bake on middle rack of the oven, uncovered, for 20 minutes, or until the cornbread topping is golden brown and firm to the touch. The sides will

be bubbling. Remove from the oven and let rest for 10 minutes before serving. There should be remaining Creole sauce that can be heated and served over the top of each portion of lasagna.

8 fresh or dry lasagna noodles

3 tablespoons Thai fish sauce

3 tablespoons fresh lime juice

2 tablespoons sugar

1 tablespoon sesame oil

1 tablespoon olive oil

4 green onions, sliced diagonally

1/2 cup shredded carrot

2 cloves garlic, minced

1 1/2 cups bean sprouts

1 (1 1/2 pound) head bok choy, cleaned and trimmed, cut in half lengthwise and then chopped

1/4 teaspoon red pepper flakes

1 tablespoon fresh cilantro, chopped, plus additional left whole for garnish

2 tablespoons chopped dry roasted peanuts

2 pounds soft tofu, drained

2 tablespoons fresh Italian parsley, minced

2 tablespoons fresh basil, minced

1/2 teaspoon turmeric

2 tablespoons Thai curry paste

1/4 cup coconut milk, not shaken

2 tablespoons sugar

Preheat oven to 400°F. Oil the bottom and sides of a 9 × 13-inch baking dish. In a large pot of boiling, salted water cook the lasagna noodles, 10 minutes for dry and 2 to 3 minutes for fresh. Remove the noodles from the water and rinse in cold water. Place the noodles on a paper towel to dry. In a small mixing bowl, combine the fish sauce, lime juice, and sugar; set the mixture aside. Heat the sesame and olive oils in a large skillet over medium to high heat. Add the onion, carrots, and garlic, and stir-fry the vegetables until tender, about 2 minutes, being careful not to brown them.

Add the bean sprouts and bok choy, combine, and cook for an additional 2 to 4 minutes until wilted. Add the pepper flakes, cilantro, and peanuts, and cook for 1 additional minute. Add the fish sauce mixture, combine, and cook until the liquid is reduced by half, about 5 minutes.

Place the tofu in the bowl of a food processor fitted with the blade attachment. Process the tofu until a uniform creamy texture is obtained. Add the parsley, basil, turmeric, curry paste, coconut milk, and sugar. Process until well combined. Remove the mixture from the processor and set it aside.

[To assemble]
Place two sheets of pasta on the bottom of your baking dish, cutting them to fit if necessary. Top with the vegetable mixture, then another layer of pasta, then the tofu mixture. Repeat the layers with pasta, vegetable mixture, pasta, and finally the tofu mixture on top. Place in the oven and bake for 20 minutes, or until it begins to turn golden brown and crack. Remove from the oven and let rest for 10 minutes before cutting to serve.

[serves 6]

Thai Lasagna with Stir-Fried Vegetables and Curried Tofu

Here I have combined all the flavors of Pad Thai with crisp, fresh Asian vegetables and a creamy tofu filling to create a truly Eastern approach to lasagna.

While preparing sautéed baby spinach and arugula one evening, I chose to add some finely chopped artichoke hearts with feta and olives. This was a hit and subsequently became a filling for this tremendous lasagna. The flavors are intense and rich, with beautiful layers of varied ingredients.

[serves 8]

Lasagna **with Artichokes and Sautéed Greens**

2 medium bunches arugula, trimmed, washed, and chopped

2 (10-ounce) bags baby spinach, trimmed, washed, and chopped

2 medium bunches Swiss chard, trimmed, washed, and chopped

9 pasta noodles

1/4 cup olive oil

4 garlic cloves, thinly sliced

8 anchovy fillets, chopped

1/4 cup white wine

1/2 cup black olives, sliced

1/4 cup Kalamata olives, sliced

1/2 cup toasted pine nuts

2 (12-ounce) jars marinated artichoke hearts, drained and chopped

2 fresh tomatoes, seeded and chopped

2 tablespoons fresh marjoram leaves, chopped

1/4 teaspoon coarse ground black pepper

1/4 teaspoon cayenne pepper

salt to taste

2 cups mascarpone cheese

1 cup heavy cream

1 cup toasted bread crumbs

1/4 cup fresh Romano or Parmesan cheese, grated

Preheat oven to 425°F. Evenly coat the bottom and sides of a 9 × 13-inch baking dish with cooking spray or olive oil. In a large pot of boiling, salted water, add the greens and blanch for 1 minute. Remove the greens from the water (reserving the water to cook the pasta in) and rinse it under cold water. Drain the greens well, squeezing out any excess water. Chop the greens into small pieces. In the same pot of boiling, salted water cook the pasta noodles for 10 minutes until al dente. Remove the pasta from the water and rinse it with cold water. Place the noodles on a towel to dry. In a large skillet, heat the olive oil over medium heat. Add the garlic and anchovies, cooking them for 1 minute, being sure to break up the anchovies with a spoon as they cook. Increase the heat to medium to high, add the greens, and sauté for 4 minutes. Add the wine and let it boil away. Add the black and Kalamata olives,

toasted pine nuts, artichoke hearts, tomatoes, marjoram leaves, black pepper, cayenne pepper, and salt if needed. Mix well and set aside. In a small saucepan, heat the mascarpone cheese with the cream over very low heat, until it just reaches a pourable consistency, about 1 minute. Remove the saucepan from the heat and season with salt and black pepper.

[To assemble]
Pour a thin layer of the mascarpone cream over the bottom of the baking dish. Add a layer of lasagna noodles, topping this with a layer of the greens mixture and a drizzle of mascarpone cream. Layer with more lasagna noodles, and top with the remaining greens and another drizzle of cream. End with pasta, the remaining cream, and an even sprinkling of toasted bread crumbs. Cover with aluminum foil and bake for 20 minutes. Uncover and continue to bake for an additional 15 minutes to brown the top. Remove from the oven and let stand for 10 minutes. Serve with freshly grated Romano or Parmesan cheese.

Tips on Toasting Nuts

Toasting nuts is simple. Whether on the stove top or in the oven, toasting is quick and produces an intensely concentrated flavor in the nuts that imparts a great, exotic flavor to many dishes. Be careful to watch the nuts closely. This is the only tricky part, because they toast very quickly.

On the stove top, place the nuts in a medium skillet over medium to high heat, tossing them in the pan continuously. The nuts will begin to brown and you will smell a nutty aroma. Remove them from the heat, place them on a dish, and let them cool.

To toast in the oven, preheat the oven to 400°F, and place the nuts on a cookie sheet. Bake for about 5 minutes (time will vary depending on the nuts used). The nuts will begin to turn golden brown and exude a nutty aroma. Remove the pan from the oven and place the nuts on a separate dish to cool.

[Two important things to remember]

1. Oil is not needed to toast nuts, because their natural oils will assist in the process.
2. Removing the nuts immediately from the skillet or cookie sheet is important so they don't continue to cook and burn. Remember, nuts have natural oils that have been heated up. When oil is hot, it cooks. The nuts can turn dark and burn before you know it.

2 tablespoons extra-virgin
olive oil

8 lasagna noodles, cooked to
al dente

1 pound mushrooms (such as
cremini or Bella), stems
removed, cleaned, and finely
chopped in a food processor

1/4 cup shallots, finely chopped

2 cloves garlic, minced

salt and coarse ground black
pepper

1 (10-ounce) package frozen
chopped spinach, defrosted
and squeezed dry

1/4 teaspoon ground nutmeg

2 cups ricotta cheese

1 cup chicken broth

8 ounces Gorgonzola cheese,
crumbled

1/2 cup heavy cream

2 tablespoons Italian
parsley, minced

1 tablespoon fresh rosemary,
chopped

1 1/2 cups shredded mozzarella

1/4 cup freshly grated Parmesan
cheese

Preheat oven to 400°F. Oil the bottom and sides of a 9 × 13-inch baking dish. In a large pot of boiling, salted water, cook the lasagna noodles until al dente, about 10 minutes. Remove the noodles from the water and rinse under cold water to cool. Set aside to dry.

Heat the olive oil in a medium skillet over medium to high heat. Sauté the mushrooms, shallots, and garlic until the mushrooms give off their juices and darken, and the shallots are tender, about 7 to 8 minutes. Season with salt and black pepper. Add the spinach, heat through for 2 additional minutes, add the nutmeg, and combine. Add the ricotta cheese, and stir into the mixture to heat the cheese through, about 1 additional minute. Remove the pan from the heat but leave the mixture in the warm skillet.

In a small saucepan, heat the broth over medium to high heat. Add the Gorgonzola to the broth and melt it. Bring the liquid to a slow boil, and stir in the cream, cooking to thicken for about 2 minutes. Add the parsley and rosemary.

[To assemble]
Place cooked, dry lasagna noodles on a large, clean work surface. Spread an even layer of spinach filling down each lasagna noodle. Create the roulade by rolling the pasta, starting from one end and rolling tight to the other. Arrange the eight bundles, seam-side down, in a baking dish. Pour warm Gorgonzola sauce over roulades and top with mozzarella. Bake for 15 minutes or until the tops are golden brown. Heat the roulades under the broiler if necessary to brown the tops. Remove from oven and let rest for 10 minutes. Serve with freshly grated Parmesan cheese.

[serves 8]

Spinach and Mushroom Lasagna **Roulades with Gorgonzola Cream**

Rolling lasagna noodles with a delicious filling is an easy way to bring an elegant twist to a traditional dish. Generally any filling will work, just make sure that plenty of sauce is used on the top and bottom to prevent the noodles from drying out during baking.

FOR HEARTY MEAT SAUCE:

2 tablespoons olive oil

1/3 pound ground beef

1/3 pound ground turkey

1/3 pound ground pork breakfast sausage seasoned with sage

salt

freshly ground black pepper

2 medium onions, finely chopped

2 stalks celery, finely chopped

1 large carrot, finely chopped

2 tablespoons chopped garlic

2 (28-ounce) cans peeled, seeded, and chopped tomatoes

1 (6-ounce) can tomato paste

1 quart beef stock or water

2 sprigs fresh thyme

2 bay leaves

3 teaspoons dried oregano or marjoram

3 teaspoons dried basil leaves

pinch of crushed red pepper

1/4 cup Parmigiano-Reggiano cheese

FOR CHEESE AND PASTA:

1 tablespoon olive oil

2 cups fresh ricotta cheese

6 ounces grated provolone cheese

8 ounces grated mozzarella cheese

1/4 cup grated Romano cheese

2 eggs

1/4 cup milk

2 tablespoons fresh basil, chopped

1 tablespoon chopped garlic

salt

Freshly ground black pepper

8 ounces grated Parmigiano-Reggiano cheese

1 (16-ounce) package of dried lasagna noodles, cooked according to package instructions

[serves 8]

Lasagna **with Hearty Meat Sauce**

A hearty dish for a cold winter night, this dish uses pork sausage and ground turkey as part of the meat sauce, with provolone cheese to round out the cheese filling.

[To prepare the meat sauce]
In a large, nonreactive saucepan, over medium heat, add the oil. When the oil is hot, add the meat and brown for 4 to 6 minutes. Season with salt and pepper, and mix well. Add the onions, celery, and carrot. Cook for 4 to 5 minutes or until the vegetables are soft. Add the garlic and tomatoes. Season with salt and pepper. Continue to cook for 2 to 3 minutes. In a medium-sized mixing bowl, whisk the tomato paste with the stock until combined. Add the canned tomatoes to the stock and paste mixture. Add the thyme, bay leaves, oregano, basil, and red pepper. Mix well. Bring the liquid to a boil, reduce the heat to medium, and simmer for about 2 hours. Stir occasionally and add more liquid if needed. During the last 30 minutes of cooking, reseason with salt and pepper and stir in the cheese. Remove from the heat and let sit for 25 minutes before serving.

[To cook pasta and cheese]
Preheat the oven to 350°F. Coat the sides and bottom of a 9 × 13-inch baking dish with 1 tablespoon of olive oil. In a large stockpot with ample salted, boiling water, cook the lasagna noodles according to the package directions. In a mixing bowl, combine the ricotta, provolone, mozzarella, grated Romano, eggs, milk, basil, and garlic. Mix well. Season with salt and pepper.

[To assemble]
Spread 1 cup of the meat sauce onto the bottom of the baking dish. Sprinkle one quarter of the Parmigiano-Reggiano cheese over the sauce. Cover the cheese with one quarter of the cooked noodles. Spread one quarter of the cheese filling evenly over the noodles. Repeat the above process with the remaining ingredients, topping the lasagna with the remaining sauce. Place in the oven and bake until bubbly and golden, about 45 minutes to 1 hour. Remove from the oven and let rest for 10 minutes before serving. Slice and serve.

4 tablespoons olive oil

1 pound fresh pasta sheets or 1 pound dried lasagna noodles, cooked according to package directions

salt and pepper

24 fresh sea scallops, cleaned

2 cups teardrop or pear tomatoes, red or yellow, cut in half lengthwise

1 pound fresh asparagus, trimmed and blanched

1 pound fresh shiitake or chanterelle mushrooms, cleaned

1 recipe Basic Pesto (page 118)

1/4 cup grated Parmigiano-Reggiano cheese

Parsley leaves for garnish

[serves 8]

Folded Lasagna with Grilled Sea Scallops

A simple "pile" of lasagna noodles makes up the basis of the dish, with succulent grilled scallops lying atop and nestled in between the folded ribbons of pasta. While far removed from the traditional idea of lasagna layers, this dish exemplifies the importance of pesto in Italian cooking.

Bring a pot of salted water to a boil with 1 tablespoon of olive oil. If using fresh pasta, boil for approximately 2 minutes until al dente. If using dry, packaged pasta, cook according to package instructions. Remove the noodles from the water and drain. In a mixing bowl, toss the pasta with a tablespoon of the remaining olive oil. Season with salt and pepper. Set aside.

Preheat the grill. Season the scallops with a tablespoon of olive oil, salt, and pepper. Place the scallops on the grill and cook for 2 to 3 minutes on each side or until the scallops are firm to the touch. In a sauté pan, over medium heat, add the remaining tablespoon of the oil.

When the oil is hot, add the tomatoes. Sauté for 2 minutes. Add the asparagus and mushrooms. Season with salt and pepper. Continue to sauté for 3 to 4 minutes or until the mushrooms are soft.

In a large mixing bowl, toss the pasta with the vegetables and pesto. Mix well. Add the cheese and mix well. Readjust the seasonings if necessary. Mound two sheets of pasta in a ribbonlike formation in the center of each serving plate. Lay the scallops between and over the pasta noodles. Garnish with parsley and serve.

chapter 4

Vegetarian and Lighter Lasagna

Bring a large pot of lightly salted water to a boil. Add the pasta and cook for 8 to 10 minutes or until al dente; drain and pat dry on a towel. In a large bowl, combine the ricotta cheese, eggs, Parmesan cheese, parsley, basil, and ground black pepper. Stir to blend; set aside.

Heat oil in a large saucepan over high heat. Sauté the onions for about 5 minutes, stirring occasionally. Add the carrot slices and sauté for about 2 minutes. Then stir in the green bell pepper, red bell pepper, and broccoli. Stir all the ingredients together, reduce the heat to medium, and cook until tender, about 5 minutes. Scrape the veggies into the ricotta mix, and combine thoroughly. Preheat the oven to 350°F. Ladle 1 cup of spaghetti sauce into a 9 × 13-inch baking dish and spread evenly over the bottom.

Place two strips of lasagna lengthwise in the dish, then spread about 4 cups of the filling over the pasta. Sprinkle 1 cup of the mozzarella cheese over the filling; repeat the layers. Bake in preheated oven for 1 hour. Let stand about 10 to 15 minutes to firm up before serving.

2 (12-ounce) packages lasagna noodles
2 pounds ricotta cheese
4 eggs
1 cup grated Parmesan cheese
1/3 cup chopped fresh parsley
2 teaspoons dried basil
Ground black pepper to taste
1/2 cup olive oil
1 1/2 cups onion, chopped
1 cup carrots, sliced
1/2 cup green bell pepper, chopped
1/2 cup red bell pepper, chopped
1 (16-ounce) package chopped frozen broccoli, thawed and drained
3 cups Quick Tomato Sauce (page 117), Slow-Simmered Tomato Sauce (page 120), or your favorite chunky-style spaghetti sauce
2 cups shredded mozzarella cheese, divided

[serves 9]

Classic Vegetarian Lasagna

This lasagna is so easy to prepare. In a culture where there are few options for vegetarians, this one is a great meatless choice. With a generous amount of garden-fresh vegetables, this lasagna goes well with a salad and warm bread to make a hearty meal.

1 tablespoon extra-virgin olive oil

1/2 cup onion, finely chopped

1/4 cup celery, finely chopped

1/4 cup carrot, finely chopped

2 garlic cloves, minced

1/2 teaspoon dried thyme

2 pounds chopped plum tomatoes (about 4 cups)

1/3 cup plus 2 tablespoons fresh basil, chopped

salt and pepper

1 cup low-fat ricotta cheese

1/2 cup packed, grated low-fat mozzarella cheese, divided

pepper

8 fresh lasagna noodles, cooked and cut in half crosswise

1/4 cup freshly grated Parmesan cheese

In a large skillet, heat the oil over medium heat. Add the onions, celery, carrot, garlic, and thyme, and sauté until the vegetables are tender and translucent, about 8 minutes. Add tomatoes with any juices; simmer until slightly thickened, about 8 minutes. Stir in 1/3 cup basil. Season with salt and pepper. In a small saucepan over medium-low heat, stir the ricotta cheese until just heated through. Add 1/4 cup packed mozzarella cheese. Stir just until melted, about 1 minute. Season to taste with pepper. Preheat broiler to high.

Spoon 1/4 cup tomato sauce into the bottom of each of four shallow bowls. Place two hot lasagna noodle halves side by side atop the sauce in each bowl. Top with one quarter of the cheese mixture, then with two more noodle halves. Divide the remaining sauce among the bowls. Sprinkle with Parmesan and remaining mozzarella cheese and 2 tablespoons basil. Place in the oven on the middle rack under the broiler for about 3 minutes until the mozzarella cheese begins to brown and bubble. Serve immediately in individual dishes.

[serves 4]

Classic Low-fat Lasagna

Even with the use of lighter ingredients, this combination has a great flavor. This lasagna is not only easy on the waistline—it also beats the clock. There is no bake time, so it takes hardly any time to prepare.

In a large bowl, combine eggplant, zucchini, peppers, onions, garlic, rosemary, 1/2 cup basil, salt, pepper, and 1/2 cup olive oil, and marinate for 2 to 3 hours at room temperature.

Preheat oven to 375°F. Remove the vegetables from the marinade to a deep roasting pan. Roast in the oven until tender and browned, about 30 minutes, stirring twice during roasting time. In a skillet, heat 2 tablespoons of olive oil. Add the mushrooms and sauté over medium heat for 3 minutes; add the baby spinach, sautéing until wilted and tender; set aside.

In a large pot of boiling, salted water, cook the lasagna noodles until al dente, 10 minutes for dry, 2 to 3 minutes for fresh. Drain and rinse with cold water. Dry on a towel.

[To assemble]
Pour 1 cup of the Béchamel Sauce over the bottom of an oiled 9 × 13-inch baking dish, and arrange about one quarter of the roasted vegetable mixture on top. Cover with pasta, then top with one quarter more of vegetable mixture, add some mushrooms, some diced tomatoes, 1/2 cup Béchamel Sauce, some of the remaining basil, and 1/2 cup Parmesan cheese. Repeat the procedure two times, ending with Parmesan cheese and 1/2 cup Béchamel Sauce. Cover with aluminum foil and bake for 25 minutes. Remove the foil and bake for an additional 10 minutes until the lasagna is bubbling and golden brown. Remove from the oven and let rest for 10 minutes before cutting to serve.

1 eggplant, peeled and chopped

2 zucchini, chopped

1 red pepper, seeded and chopped

1 yellow pepper, seeded and chopped

1 small yellow onion, chopped

2 garlic cloves, finely minced

2 sprigs rosemary

1 cup fresh basil, shredded

salt and freshly ground black pepper

2/3 cup extra-virgin olive oil

1 cup chopped fresh shiitake mushrooms

10 ounces baby spinach

9 fresh or dry lasagna noodles

3 cups Béchamel Sauce (page 113)

2 beefsteak tomatoes, peeled, seeded, and cubed

2 cups grated Parmesan cheese

[serves 6]

Vegetable Lasagna with White Sauce

Garden-fresh summer vegetables fill the layers of this vibrant vegetarian dish. The creamy Béchamel Sauce gives the lasagna the richness and moisture it needs while allowing the vegetables to take center stage.

9 lasagna noodles, dried or fresh

1 tablespoon unsalted butter

2 tablespoons olive oil

2 shallots, chopped

3 cloves garlic, minced

1 medium carrot, chopped

1 medium parsnip, chopped

10 ounces mushrooms (such as Bella or crimini), sliced thin

2 (10-ounce) packages frozen broccoli, thawed, drained, and chopped, or 1 1/2 pounds fresh broccoli, trimmed, blanched, drained, and chopped

1 tablespoon fresh Italian parsley, minced

salt and coarse ground black pepper

3 cups Béchamel Sauce (page 113)

1/2 cup milk

1 pound Fontina cheese, shredded

zest of one lemon

pinch of grated nutmeg

2 tablespoons fresh basil, chopped

1 cup grated Parmesan cheese

9 ounces goat cheese (such as Montrachet)

[serves 8]

Broccoli Lasagna with Mushrooms and Fontina Cheese

In this easy-to-prepare dish, the robust flavor of Fontina cheese lends itself well to the crisp, garden-fresh flavor of broccoli and the exotic flavors of mushrooms.

Preheat oven to 400°F. Evenly coat sides and bottom of a 9 × 13-inch baking dish with cooking spray or olive oil. In a large pot of boiling, salted water, cook the lasagna noodles until al dente, 10 minutes for dried, 2 to 3 minutes for fresh. Remove noodles from water, rinse under cold water, and set aside on a towel to dry.

Melt the butter with the olive oil in a large sauté pan over medium to high heat. Sauté the shallots with the garlic, carrot, and parsnip until the shallots begin to brown and the carrots and parsnips become tender, about 5 minutes. Add the mushrooms and continue to cook, allowing the mushrooms to sweat and wilt, about 4 minutes. Add the broccoli and parsley, stirring to combine. Continue to cook for an additional 2 minutes to heat broccoli through. Season with salt and pepper, remove from heat, and set aside. In a medium-sized saucepan, heat the Béchamel Sauce. Add 1/2 cup milk to thin, bring to a simmer, add Fontina cheese and lemon zest, and cook over medium heat, stirring constantly until smooth and creamy and Fontina cheese is melted, about 15 minutes. Season with nutmeg and salt and pepper.

[To assemble]

In the baking dish, layer 1 cup of the Fontina cheese sauce, three lasagna noodles, 1 cup more Fontina cheese sauce, half the broccoli-mushroom mixture, half the chopped basil, one third of the Parmesan cheese, and one third of the goat cheese. Top with three additional noodles, half of the remaining Fontina cheese sauce, remaining broccoli-mushroom mixture, remaining basil, one third of the Parmesan cheese, and one third of the goat cheese. Top with remaining three noodles and Fontina cheese sauce, then sprinkle with the remaining Parmesan and goat cheese. Cover with foil coated with cooking spray. Bake for 20 minutes, uncover, and bake for an additional 10 to 15 minutes until top is golden and bubbly. Remove from oven and let rest for 10 minutes before cutting to serve.

Roasted Asparagus Lasagna with Fontina Cheese

Fresh, oven-roasted asparagus is a favorite of mine with any dish. In this lasagna, I have combined the rich flavors of Parmigiano cream sauce and Fontina cheese with the intense flavors of roasted asparagus and onions.

2 1/2 pounds medium asparagus, ends trimmed, stalks peeled, and cut in half

1 large Vidalia or sweet onion, peeled, cut in half, and thinly sliced

3 tablespoons extra-virgin olive oil

2 tablespoons unsalted butter

1/4 cup fresh-squeezed lemon juice

2 teaspoons grated lemon peel

salt

coarsely ground black pepper

3 fresh savory sprigs, leaves chopped

2 fresh tarragon sprigs, leaves chopped

FOR THE PARMIGIANO SAUCE:

1 cup freshly grated Parmigiano-Reggiano cheese

2 cups heavy cream

freshly grated nutmeg

3 tablespoons fresh chives, finely chopped

1 recipe Basic Pasta (page 122), cut for lasagna or 1 pound dry lasagna noodles

1/2 pound grated Fontina cheese

1/2 pound grated mozzarella cheese

Preheat the oven to 450°F. Place the asparagus and onions on a large baking sheet. Drizzle with the olive oil, and dot with the butter. Sprinkle the lemon juice and zest on top and season with salt and coarsely ground black pepper. Mix the vegetables well with your hands, making sure they are evenly coated with the seasonings. Bake until soft and just starting to brown, about 20 minutes.

When the vegetables are tender and aromatic, remove them from the oven and sprinkle with the savory and tarragon. Toss to combine. The heat of the vegetables will wilt and concentrate the flavors of the herbs.

Lower the oven temperature to 425°F. In a small saucepan, stir the Parmigiano-Reggiano cheese into the cream and mix well. Simmer gently over low heat until the cheese is melted and the sauce is fairly smooth (there will be a slight graininess to the sauce because of the texture of the cheese). Season with the nutmeg, black pepper, and a pinch of salt. Add the chives and stir. If using fresh pasta, cook the lasagna sheets in a large pot of boiling, salted water until tender, about

2 minutes. If using dry noodles, cook them according to the package directions. Drain the noodles and rinse them with cold water, then lay them out in one layer on a towel to dry.

[To assemble]
Lightly coat an 8 × 8-inch baking dish with olive oil. Layer the bottom with pasta, and follow with a layer of asparagus and onion and a thin layer of grated Fontina and mozzarella cheese. Season lightly. Add another layer of pasta, and top with more asparagus, half of the Parmigiano cream sauce, and another thin layer of Fontina and mozzarella cheeses. Repeat until you use up the ingredients, ending with a layer of pasta. Pour the remaining Parmigiano cream on top. letting it run down the sides a bit.

Cover the dish with aluminum foil and bake for about 20 minutes. Remove the foil and continue to bake until the top is golden and bubbling, about an additional 15 to 20 minutes. Remove from oven and let rest for 10 minutes before cutting.

[Variations]
Roasting vegetables concentrates and intensifies their flavors. Vegetables such as eggplant, butternut squash, leeks, peppers, tomatoes, and artichoke hearts are all great choices for roasting. Simply coat them in olive oil, toss with salt and black pepper, and roast in a hot oven until tender and brown. Layer in lasagna with Quick Tomato Sauce (page 117) or with the Parmigiano cream sauce and cheeses in this recipe.

For an incredible variation in flavors, replace either the Fontina or mozzarella cheese with their smoked counterpart. Smoking cheese intensifies the flavors of the cheese, much as roasting vegetables does. In addition, it gives the cheese an earthy flavor of smoke.

A note on fresh herbs

Fresh herbs are like gold to any seasoned cook. The flavors and variations are endless. The contribution that fresh herbs make to any dish are irreplaceable. Unfortunately, fresh herbs are not always available, depending on the time of year and your location or available supermarkets. When you can find fresh herbs, they can be easily frozen for later use. Simply wash and clean the herbs thoroughly, being sure to pick any dead or rotting leaves form the bunch. Dry the herbs completely, layer on a paper towel in a single layer, and roll the paper towel from end to end tightly. Place them in an airtight container or freezer bag and freeze for later use. I do not suggest using frozen herbs in fresh sauces such as pesto, however; make the pesto when fresh herbs are available and freeze it.

In the case of basil and hard-stemmed, broad-leaved herbs, remove the leaves from the steams, freezing only the leaves of the plant.

Substituting herbs
[Dried for fresh]

In some cases, dried herbs are needed when fresh are not available. When using dried herbs, remember one simple rule: Use half as much of the dried as you would of the fresh. The flavors of dried herbs are concentrated and harsher than those of fresh, so less is needed.

[One herb for another]

Sometimes, when a recipe calls for one herb that is not available fresh, but dried is not preferred, there may be a fresh herb that can be substituted. For example, in the recipe for Roasted Asparagus Lasagna with Fontina Cheese, savory and tarragon are called for. In this case, if one or the other is not available, just increase the quantity of the one that is available to equal the quantity of the two. An herb like savory is similar in smell and flavor to oregano and marjoram. So, one of those could also be substituted if the other is not available. Generally, a recipe will tell you if dried can be used or if there is an alternative to the fresh one if it is not available. If that assistance is not in the recipe, then ask your local grocer.

2 summer squash (approx. 1¼ pounds)

2 zucchini (approx. 1¼ pounds)

5 large carrots, peeled

¼ cup plus 2 tablespoons extra-virgin olive oil

1 tablespoon black pepper

1 medium eggplant

2 portobello mushrooms, stems removed, wiped clean with a damp cloth

FOR THE CHEESE FILLING:

1 pound ricotta cheese, whole milk or part skim

8 ounces feta cheese, crumbled

½ cup packed fresh basil leaves, sliced thinly

1 egg

1 pound fresh or packaged dry lasagna noodles

1 recipe Fire Roasted Red Pepper Sauce (page 114)

6 ounces packaged baby spinach

8 ounces shredded mozzarella cheese

[serves 9]

Grilled Vegetable Lasagna **with Fire-Roasted Red Pepper Sauce**

I love to grill vegetables no matter the occasion or time of year. While it is a bit more time-consuming, the taste is tremendous. There is no substitute for the intensity that fire imparts to the flavors of vegetables.

[To prepare the vegetables]
Wash and clean all the vegetables, and slice the squash, zucchini, and carrots diagonally about ¼ inch thick. In a large bowl, toss the sliced squash, zucchini, and carrots with 2 tablespoons olive oil and 1 tablespoon black pepper, coating it evenly. Set aside. Peel the eggplant and slice it into ¼-inch-thick rounds. Place the eggplant and the whole mushrooms on a plate and coat them evenly with the remaining ¼ cup of olive oil. On a hot outdoor grill or stove-top grill pan, grill the vegetables.

Grill the squash, zucchini, carrots, and eggplant for about 7 minutes on each side; grill the mushrooms for about 20 minutes on each side. Grilling times will vary depending on the cooking surface and the appliance.

When grilling is complete, set all the vegetables aside for assembly, except the mushrooms. The mushrooms need to be sliced thinly for assembly.

[To prepare the cheese filling]
In a large mixing bowl, combine the ricotta cheese, feta cheese, basil, and egg. Set aside.

[To assemble]
Preheat the oven to 350°F. Oil the bottom and sides of a 9 × 13-inch baking dish.

If using store-bought dry noodles, prepare them according to package directions. If using fresh pasta, boil it in an

ample amount of boiling, salted water for 2 to 3 minutes. Remove the noodles from the water and run them under cold water until cooled. Set aside on paper towels to dry. Using about 1/2 cup red pepper sauce, evenly coat the bottom of the baking dish. Top the sauce with an even layer of lasagna noodles, being careful not to overlap them. Cut the lasagna noodles to fit the pan if necessary. Top the pasta with half of the baby spinach in an even layer, then with half of the vegetables, alternating the vegetables in an even layer. Top the vegetables with a sprinkling of half of the mozzarella cheese, then with another layer of lasagna noodles. Evenly coat the noodles with half of the ricotta cheese mixture. Top with another layer of lasagna noodles, then the remaining spinach, grilled vegetables, and mozzarella cheese. Add three additional lasagna noodles. Top the lasagna with the remaining red pepper sauce. Cover the pan and bake for 30 minutes. Uncover and bake an additional 15 to 20 minutes until the sauce is browned.

2 pounds broccoli rabe

3 tablespoons olive oil

1 cup ricotta cheese

$1/2$ cup feta cheese

$1/4$ teaspoon dried oregano
leaves

$1/2$ teaspoon fresh rosemary
leaves

$1/8$ teaspoon freshly grated
nutmeg

3 egg whites

1 egg yolk

$1/4$ cup milk, whole or low-fat

$1/2$ cup bread crumbs

salt and pepper

1 pound lasagna noodles

$1/2$ cup extra-virgin olive oil

4 cups Béchamel Sauce (page 113)

1 tablespoon olive oil

$1/2$ cup freshly grated
Parmesan cheese

$1/2$ cup butter or margarine

[To prepare the rabe]

Wash and clean the rabe carefully. Chop the rabe coarsely. In a large pan, sauté the rabe in 3 tablespoons of olive oil for about 5 minutes until it is tender and bright green in color. Remove the rabe from the heat and place it in a colander over the sink to drain. Chop the rabe either by hand or in a food processor so that it is chopped very fine but not puréed.

[To prepare the remainder of the filling]

Place the chopped rabe in a large mixing bowl. Add the ricotta cheese, feta cheese, oregano, rosemary, grated nutmeg, egg whites and yolk, and milk. Mix thoroughly. Add the bread crumbs and combine. Set aside for 10 to 15 minutes, while the bread crumbs absorb the liquids. Check the consistency after this time, adding water or bread crumbs, depending upon whether the mixture seems too loose or too dry. Season it with salt and pepper.

While the mixture is resting, cook the lasagna noodles in a large amount of water with salt and oil, according to the package directions. Once they are al dente, drain them and mix them with the olive oil to keep them from sticking together.

[To assemble]

Preheat the oven to 350°F. Grease the bottom and sides of a 9 × 13-inch baking dish. Place one layer of noodles on the bottom of the dish and cover with about ½ inch of the filling mixture. Ladle about ½ cup of Béchamel Sauce over the noodles, and sprinkle freshly grated Parmesan cheese over this layer. Cover with another layer of noodles. Repeat the process by alternating layers of noodles, filling, and Béchamel Sauce until the dish is full, with the last layer being noodles. Sprinkle olive oil and Parmesan cheese on the top. Dot with butter and bake for 45 minutes. Remove from the oven. Let rest for 10 to 15 minutes before slicing to serve. Cover each lasagna serving with warmed Béchamel Sauce.

[serves 6 to 8]

Broccoli Rabe Lasagna

Broccoli rabe has a bitter taste that's not for every palate. In this dish, I have added fresh herbs and nutmeg to balance the flavor of the rabe and have used feta cheese to impart a creamy, exotic flavor.

When developing this recipe, I wanted to combine
the garden-fresh flavors of greens with the crisp textures
of spring vegetables. Instead of a typical ricotta cheese
layer, I created a risotto-style filling with fresh herbs and
goat cheese.

[serves 8]

Spring Vegetable Lasagna
with Herbed Cream

FOR VEGETABLE FILLING:

2 tablespoons unsalted butter

2 tablespoons olive oil

2 cups fresh zucchini, finely chopped

1 cup asparagus, trimmed, cut into 1-inch lengths

2 cups fresh fennel bulbs, finely chopped

1 medium onion, finely chopped

1 cup carrot, finely chopped

4 cloves garlic, minced

2 cups shiitake mushrooms, thinly sliced

1 cup raddichio, finely shredded

salt and coarsely ground black pepper

16 ounces fresh baby spinach

FOR RISOTTO FILLING:

1 tablespoon unsalted butter

1 tablespoon olive oil

1 cup Arborio rice

1 cup dry white wine

4 cups chicken or vegetable stock or canned broth

2 tablespoons minced Italian parsley

$1/2$ cup freshly grated Parmigiano-Reggiano cheese

$3^1/2$ ounces goat cheese

salt and coarsely ground black pepper

FOR HERBED CREAM:

4 tablespoons unsalted butter

4 tablespoons all-purpose flour

$1/2$ cup dry white wine

2 cups chicken or vegetable stock or canned broth

3 tablespoons fresh basil, minced

2 tablespoons fresh tarragon, minced

3 tablespoons fresh chives, minced

1 tablespoon fennel tops, minced

1 teaspoon orange zest, minced

1 cup heavy cream

Salt and coarsely ground black pepper

TO ASSEMBLE:

12 sheets fresh or dried lasagna noodles

10 ounces fresh mozzarella cheese, sliced thinly

Preheat oven to 400°F. Evenly coat a 9 × 13-inch baking dish with cooking spray or olive oil. In a large pot of salted, boiling water, cook the noodles, 10 minutes for dried or 2 to 3 minutes for fresh. Remove from water, rinse under cold water, drain, and set aside on paper towels to dry. For vegetable filling, melt 1 tablespoon butter with 1 tablespoon olive oil in a large skillet over medium to high heat. Sauté zucchini, asparagus, fennel, onion, carrot, and garlic until tender and just beginning to color, about 15 minutes. Add shiitake mushrooms and radicchio. Combine and cook until wilted, about 3 minutes. Season with salt and pepper. Remove from heat and transfer to a platter. In the same skillet, heat the remaining tablespoon of butter and oil. Add the baby spinach, stirring to heat and wilt, about 2 minutes. Remove from heat and transfer to a platter.

[For risotto]

Melt butter with olive oil in a medium skillet over medium to high heat. Add the rice, coating it with butter and oil, stirring constantly to lightly brown, about 5 minutes. Add the wine and incorporate. Cook until all the wine has evaporated, about 5 minutes. Begin adding chicken stock to pan 1/2 cup at a time. Between additions of stock, cook until it has evaporated, stirring periodically to combine. The rice will begin to plump up and become tender. Continue this process of adding stock and cooking until all the stock has been used up. At this time, the risotto should have almost tripled in volume and be very fluffy and tender with a creamy consistency. If not, continue to add water or stock until a creamy consistency is reached. Remove from heat and transfer to a bowl. Add the parsley, Parmigiano-Reggiano, and goat cheese. Stir to combine and melt cheeses. Add the salt and pepper to taste. Set aside to cool.

[For herbed cream]

Melt butter in a medium-sized saucepan over medium to high heat. Add flour and whisk to combine. Whisk continuously, cooking flour to a golden brown color. Combine the wine and stock together in a bowl. Gradually add the wine and stock mixture to the flour mixture, whisking constantly to combine. Add the liquid slowly to prevent lumps. Be careful of the steam that will rise from the pan at the initial addition of the liquid. After the addition of all the wine-stock mixture, add the basil, tarragon, chives, fennel tops, and orange zest. Stir to combine. Lower the heat to medium and continue to cook for about 2 minutes. Add the cream and simmer for 5 additional minutes. Season with salt and pepper. Remove from the heat.

[To assemble lasagna]

Begin with about 1 cup of herbed cream on the bottom of the baking dish. Top with three sheets of noodles, and layer with half of the spinach, then half of the vegetable mixture. Top the vegetables with 1 cup of herbed cream, and add one third of the mozzarella cheese. Repeat with three pasta noodles. Add all of the risotto mixture in an even layer. If the risotto appears to be too dry after cooling, add about 1/4 cup of heavy cream or milk to it to moisten it. Top the risotto with another layer of three noodles. Layer with remaining spinach, remaining vegetable mixture, about 1 cup of herbed cream, and one third of the fresh mozzarella. Top with the last three noodles, then add the remaining herbed cream, finishing with the remaining mozzarella cheese. Bake uncovered for 30 minutes or until the top is bubbling and golden brown. Remove from the oven and let rest for 10 minutes before cutting to serve.

2 tablespoons olive oil

1 medium yellow onion, thinly sliced

2 tablespoons garlic, minced

10 Roma tomatoes, seeded, cut into chunks (1 1/2 pounds)

2 teaspoons fresh rosemary, minced

1 teaspoon fresh oregano, minced

2 tablespoons fresh basil, minced

1 tablespoon butter

1/2 cup toasted bread crumbs

6 dried lasagna noodles, cooked according to package instructions

4 russet potatoes, sliced 1/8 inch thick

salt and pepper

1 cup grated Swiss cheese

1 cup grated Gruyere cheese

Preheat oven to 450°F. Spray a 9 × 13-inch baking dish with cooking spray. Sauté the onions in a skillet over medium-high heat with olive oil until just soft. Stir in the garlic, and cook another minute until just aromatic. Add the tomatoes, rosemary, oregano, and basil. Continue to cook until all moisture has evaporated, about 10 minutes.

[Toasting bread crumbs]
In a skillet (preferably Teflon-coated), melt 1 tablespoon butter. Add the bread crumbs and combine, stirring to coat evenly while cooking. Cook until golden brown and aromatic, about 5 minutes. Remove from the heat and allow to cool.

[To assemble]
Layer one third of the lasagna noodles in the prepared casserole dish. Top with half of the sliced potatoes, and season with salt and pepper. Top the potatoes with half of the tomato mixture, and sprinkle with half the cheeses. Repeat the layering, ending with cheese. Sprinkle evenly with toasted bread crumbs. Cover the gratin with foil and bake for 30 minutes. Remove the foil and bake for an additional 15 to 20 minutes to brown the cheese. Let stand 5 minutes to set the cheese before slicing and serving.

[serves 6 as a meal or 8 as a side dish]

Potato Gratin Lasagna

This is an adaptation of a great vegetable side dish. The lasagna noodles give it more layers and a firm consistency. Cut it into smaller portions and serve it as a side with roasted chicken. Larger portions served with a salad make a great vegetarian meal.

Preheat oven to 400°F. Combine the mushrooms, onion, garlic, basil, and parsley in a large baking dish. Drizzle with olive oil. Toss everything with your hands to coat evenly and combine. Top with chunks of butter. Pour the chicken broth over the vegetables, then add the cayenne pepper and coriander. Place in the oven and cook, uncovered, until the vegetables are tender and beginning to brown, about 20 to 30 minutes. Remove from the heat and set aside. In a large mixing bowl, combine the Asiago and mozzarella cheese and set it aside.

[To assemble]
In a well-oiled 9 × 13-inch baking dish, place 1 cup of the Quick Tomato Sauce on the bottom. Top with three lasagna noodles, and place half of the mushroom mixture on top of the noodles, topping with half of the arugula and then with about one third of the shredded cheeses. Top the cheeses with pasta noodles, add 1½ cups sauce, and repeat the layers with the remaining mushroom mixture, one third of the cheeses, and the remaining arugula. Add the remaining three lasagna noodles, and top with the remaining tomato sauce and cheeses. Place in the oven and bake until bubbly and golden, about 45 minutes.

3 pounds portobello mushrooms, sliced

1 large onion, cut in half and sliced thinly

3 cloves garlic, minced

¼ cup fresh basil, thinly sliced

2 tablespoons Italian parsley, minced

4 tablespoons extra-virgin olive oil

2 tablespoons unsalted butter

1 cup chicken broth

½ teaspoon cayenne pepper

½ teaspoon ground coriander

8 ounces Asiago cheese, shredded

8 ounces mozzarella cheese, shredded

2 cups Quick Tomato Sauce (page 117)

1 pound lasagna noodles cooked according to package instructions

[serves 9]

Roasted Portobello and Caramelized Onion Lasagna

This is a light dish with the robust, earthy flavors of roasted portobello mushrooms. The only cheeses in this dish are the shredded Asiago and mozzarella. There is no heavy layer of ricotta or creamy sauce, just fresh mushrooms and arugula.

2 teaspoons olive oil

3 cups chopped leeks (about 4)

1 tablespoon chopped fresh or
1 teaspoon dried rubbed sage

4 garlic cloves, minced

5 cups peeled butternut squash
in 1/2-inch cubes

1/2 cup dry white wine

1/2 cup water

1/4 teaspoon black pepper

1 (10-ounce) package frozen
chopped spinach, thawed,
drained, and squeezed dry

FOR THE SAUCE:

2 tablespoons unsalted butter
or margarine

3 tablespoons all-purpose flour

2 1/2 cups milk

1/4 cup block-style cream cheese

1/4 teaspoon ground nutmeg

1/8 teaspoon black pepper

1 1/4 cups mozzarella cheese

3/4 cup shredded sharp
provolone cheese

12 cooked lasagna noodles

sage sprigs for garnish

[To prepare vegetable filling]
Heat the oil in a large, nonstick skillet over medium heat. Add the leeks, sage, and garlic. Sauté 5 minutes. Add the squash, wine, and water. Cover and cook for 20 minutes or until the squash is tender, stirring occasionally. Stir in 1/4 teaspoon pepper and the spinach.

[To prepare sauce]
In a large saucepan over medium-high heat, melt the butter, add the flour, and whisk the mixture until combined. Cook for 3 minutes to brown the flour. Gradually add the milk to the flour mixture, whisking continuously to prevent lumps. Reduce the heat to medium, and cook until thick (about 10 minutes), stirring constantly. Remove the saucepan from the heat; add the cream cheese, nutmeg, and half of the pepper, stirring with the whisk. Combine the mozzarella and provolone, and set aside.

[To assemble]
Preheat the oven to 400°F. Oil the sides and bottom of a 9 × 13-inch baking dish. Spread 1/2 cup of sauce on the bottom, arrange the noodles over the sauce, and top with 2 cups of vegetable filling, 1/2 cup of the cheese mixture, and 1/2 cup of sauce. Repeat the layers, ending with the noodles. Spread the remaining sauce over the noodles. Cover and bake for 30 minutes. Uncover, sprinkle with 1/2 cup of the cheese mixture, and bake an additional 10 minutes. Let stand for 10 minutes prior to cutting to serve. Garnish with sage sprigs, if desired.

[serves 8]

Butternut Squash and Spinach Lasagna

The best time to make this lasagna is when butternut squash is ripe—right out of the fall harvest. The creamy texture of the squash combines well with spinach and leeks in this dish.

chapter 5

Breakfast Lasagna

Preheat oven to 400°F. Coat an 8 × 8-inch baking dish with nonstick cooking spray. In a large pot of boiling, salted water, cook the lasagna noodles until al dente, 10 minutes for dried, 2 to 3 minutes for fresh. Remove from the water and rinse with cold water. Place on a towel to dry thoroughly.

In a large skillet over medium to high heat, melt 2 tablespoons butter, and add the onion, red and green pepper, and broccoli. Sauté until tender and onions are translucent, being careful not the brown them, about 10 minutes. Add the smoked ham and continue to cook for an additional 3 minutes. Season with salt and pepper. Remove from the heat and set aside.

In a small skillet over medium to high heat, melt 1 tablespoon butter. Add the potato, cooking until golden brown, about 10 minutes. Season with salt and pepper, and toss with the parsley. Remove from the heat.

In a medium bowl, beat together the eggs and the heavy cream, salt, and pepper.

[To assemble]
Place two sheets of pasta on the bottom of the baking dish, top with half of the vegetable mixture, then sprinkle with one third of the cheddar cheese. Top again with lasagna noodles, then with browned potatoes. Repeat with the noodles, the vegetable mixture, one third of the cheese, the last layer of noodles, then the bread cubes. Pour the beaten eggs over the bread cubes, and top with the remaining cheddar cheese. Bake for 40 minutes or until the egg topping is golden and firm. Remove from the oven, and let rest for 10 minutes before cutting to serve. Serve with warmed Béchamel Sauce.

8 lasagna noodles, dry or fresh

2 tablespoons butter

1/2 cup onion, chopped

1/2 cup red pepper, chopped

1/2 cup green pepper, chopped

1 cup broccoli florets, chopped small

1 pound smoked ham, sliced thickly and chopped

salt and pepper

1 tablespoon butter

1 Yukon gold or russet potato, peeled and shredded

1 teaspoon fresh Italian parsley, minced

3 eggs

2 tablespoons heavy cream

1/4 teaspoon salt

1/4 teaspoon coarsely ground black pepper

12 ounces shredded cheddar cheese

2 thick slices day-old French bread or Portuguese sweet bread, cut into 1-inch cubes, tossed with 3 tablespoons melted butter

1 1/2 cups Béchamel Sauce (page 113)

[serves 6]

Baked Egg Strata Lasagna

This is a layered take on the classic one-dish breakfast. The flavors of the vegetables layered with potatoes and cheddar are intense. Enjoy with toast and fruit.

FOR SIMPLE BUTTERMILK BISCUITS:

2 cups self-rising flour

1/4 cup shortening

1 cup buttermilk, well chilled

1/4 cup butter

FOR HAM AND GRAVY:

1 tablespoon bacon drippings or unsalted butter

6 slices moist, uncooked country ham or other smoked ham, about 1/3 inch thick

1 1/2 teaspoons unbleached all-purpose flour

1 cup fresh hot coffee

1/4 cup warm water

2 teaspoons brown sugar

Cayenne pepper to taste

Salt and freshly ground pepper

Few drops of hot sauce to taste

6 eggs, scrambled or fried

6 thin slices cheddar cheese

Preheat oven to 500°F. Combine the flour and shortening in a medium-sized mixing bowl with a pastry blender until the mixture is crumbly. Add the buttermilk, stirring just until the dry ingredients are moistened. Turn the dough out onto a lightly floured surface. Lightly dust the dough with flour, then roll or pat the dough to a 1/2-inch thickness. Cut dough with a 2 1/2-inch biscuit cutter, trying to get as many biscuits as possible, since they toughen if the dough is rerolled. Your dough should yield twelve biscuits. Do not twist the cutter (as seems to be natural for many people), as it twists the dough, resulting in an uneven biscuit. Place in a greased 9 ×13-inch baking dish. Top each unbaked biscuit with a small pat of cold butter. Bake the biscuits on the center rack of the oven for 12 to 14 minutes until raised and golden brown.

Meanwhile, in a large, heavy skillet over medium to high heat, melt the drippings. (A well-seasoned, cast-iron skillet is the preferred appliance in the South, due solely to the flavors it imparts to the gravy). Slash the edges of the ham's exterior fat to keep the slices from curling while cooking. Fry the ham slices in batches until lightly browned in spots and a bit crispy around the edges, about 2 minutes per side. Arrange the ham slices on a platter when they are done. Keep the ham warm and reserve the pan drippings in the skillet.

[serves 6]

Simple Buttermilk Biscuit Stack with Country Ham and Red-Eye Gravy

This traditional Southern breakfast is a must-have on blustery winter mornings by the fire. Red-eye gravy is a staple Georgian breakfast condiment, using a cuppa joe to liven it up!

While the biscuits are baking, finish the gravy. Reheat the pan drippings over medium heat and whisk in the flour. Pour in the coffee and scrape up any browned bits from the bottom of the skillet. Add at least $1/4$ cup of warm water; use more for a milder coffee jolt. Season the gravy with brown sugar and cayenne pepper. Taste the gravy and add salt, pepper, and hot sauce as needed.

[To assemble stacks]

Slice the biscuits in half. Place the biscuit bottoms back in the baking dish. Layer with sliced ham, cooked egg, and cheese. Place the tops of the biscuits back on. Place in the oven and bake for 10 minutes until the cheese begins to melt and run down the sides. Serve with a side of red-eye gravy.

In a medium-sized saucepan, melt 6 tablespoons of butter over medium heat. Add the walnuts to the butter and "toast" them for about 2 minutes until you smell a nutty aroma. Add the bananas, brown sugar, 1/4 cup maple syrup, 1/2 teaspoon cinnamon, and 1/4 teaspoon nutmeg. Reduce the heat to low and let the sauce cook until the bananas become tender and the sauce is thick.

In a large mixing bowl, beat together the milk, cream, eggs, remaining cinnamon, and vanilla.

Heat a lightly oiled griddle or skillet over medium-high heat. Dunk each slice of bread in the mixture, soaking both sides. Place on the griddle and cook both sides until golden brown. When serving, lay one slice of French toast on a warmed plate, top with a scoop of the banana compote, layer with another slice of bread, and repeat with banana compote. Finish with one last piece of French toast. Arrange banana slices in a flower-petal configuration, overlapping them in a circular pattern. Top with fresh whipped cream and fresh orange zest.

[Variation]
When in season, fresh blueberries are delicious. Reduce the bananas by one and add 1/2 cup fresh blueberries for a refreshing seasonal treat.

6 tablespoons unsalted butter

1/2 cup chopped walnuts

4 ripe bananas, peeled and sliced

2 tablespoons packed brown sugar

1/3 cup maple syrup plus additional for serving

1/2 teaspoon ground cinnamon plus another 1/2 teaspoon

1/4 teaspoon ground nutmeg, divided

3/4 cup milk

1/2 cup whipping cream or half-and-half

3 eggs

1 teaspoon vanilla extract

12 thin slices white bread

fresh whipped cream

orange zest

[serves 4]

French Toast Lasagna with Banana-Walnut Compote

For breakfast, the French toast replaces lasagna noodles to create this delightful comfort food. Use thinly sliced bread to achieve multiple layers while avoiding too much of a good thing.

MAKE THREE BATCHES OF
THE FOLLOWING:

3 eggs, lightly beaten

1/2 cup flour

1/4 teaspoon salt

1 cup milk

1 tablespoon fresh chives, minced

1 tablespoon fresh basil, minced

3 tablespoons butter

FOR THE FILLING:

5 tablespoons olive oil

1 tablespoon unsalted butter

3 medium ripe tomatoes, seeded
and chopped

1 medium yellow, orange, or red
pepper, chopped

10 ounces mushrooms, sliced thinly

4 scallions, sliced thinly

3 cloves fresh garlic, minced

2 tablespoons olive oil

10 ounces fresh baby spinach

1 (12-ounce) package ground
breakfast sausage

4 ounces shredded cheddar cheese

4 ounces shredded mozzarella
cheese, or 8 ounces shredded
cheddar-Jack cheese

2 tablespoons fresh Italian
parsley, minced

Preheat oven to 450°F. In a medium-sized mixing bowl, whisk the eggs with the flour until creamy and free of lumps. Add the salt and milk, 1/2 cup at a time, whisking to combine. Add the chives and basil, and incorporate them. You will need three separate batches of the egg mixture to complete the dish. Do not make three batches at once, as it is difficult to incorporate the flour all at once.

Place three 9-inch round cake pans in the oven for 5 minutes. Remove the pans from the oven, and coat them evenly with cooking spray. Add 1 tablespoon of butter to each pan, and return the pans to the oven to melt butter, about 1 to 2 minutes. Remove the pans from the oven and rotate to coat with butter. Pour the batter evenly into pans.

Return the pans to the oven and bake uncovered for 7 minutes. Reduce the heat to 350°F and bake for an additional 5 minutes until brown. The batter will become very fluffy as it bakes. When removed from the oven and allowed to rest, the omelette will fall to a thinner size. If possible, bake all three at once, so that assembly is quick.

While the batter is baking, melt the butter with the oil in a large sauté pan over medium to high heat. Sauté the tomato, peppers, mushrooms, scallions, and garlic until tender. Do not brown or overcook. The vegetables should be tender with vibrant color. Remove them from the pan and set them aside for

assembly. Heat an additional 2 tablespoons of olive oil. Add the baby spinach and heat through until wilted and vibrant green. Do not overcook. Remove it from the pan and set it aside for assembly. In the same sauté pan, brown the sausage, breaking it up as it cooks. Remove it from the heat and set it aside for assembly. In a medium-sized mixing bowl, combine the cheddar and mozzarella cheese, and parsley.

[To assemble]
Place one omelette in either a cake pan previously used for the omelette or in an ovenproof serving platter. Top the omelette with half of the spinach, then one third of the cheese mixture. Top the cheese evenly with half of the vegetable mixture, then half of the ground sausage. Place a second omelette on top. Repeat the layers with the remaining spinach, one third of the cheese, the remaining vegetables, and the sausage. Top with the third omelette, herb-side up. Finish with the remaining cheese. Place the layered dish in the oven to melt the cheeses, about 10 minutes. Use the broiler to melt the top layer of cheese, if necessary. Remove from the oven, slice into pie-shaped pieces, and serve. Accompany it with breakfast potatoes and juice.

[serves 6 to 8]

Baked Omelette Lasagna

This is probably the most hearty breakfast dish I have seen in a while. Thick layers of fluffy herbed omelettes with sautéed vegetables and melted cheese make this a towering breakfast meal.

chapter 6

Dessert Lasagna

6 dried lasagna noodles

8 Gala or Golden Delicious apples, cored, peeled, and sliced

2/3 cup all-purpose flour, divided

1/2 cup packed brown sugar, divided

1 1/2 teaspoons cinnamon, divided

3/4 teaspoon nutmeg, divided

2 cups ricotta cheese

2 cups cheddar cheese, shredded

1 egg

1 teaspoon vanilla extract

1/3 cup old-fashioned oats

3 tablespoons unsalted butter or margarine

1 cup sugar, divided

Cook the noodles according to the package directions, then drain. Preheat the oven to 350°F. In a large bowl, mix the apples, 1/3 cup flour, 3/4 cup brown sugar, 1 teaspoon cinnamon, and 1/2 teaspoon nutmeg. In another bowl mix the cheeses and the egg. Spread half of the apple filling over bottom of a 9 × 13-inch baking dish. Layer with three noodles, then the cheese mixture. Layer again with the remaining noodles and apple filling.

Wipe out the medium-sized bowl and use it to mix the oats, remaining 1/3 cup flour, 1/4 cup brown sugar, 1 cup sugar, 1/2 teaspoon cinnamon, and 1/4 teaspoon nutmeg. Using a pastry cutter or your fingers, cut in the butter until the mixture is crumbly. Sprinkle it evenly over the top of the lasagna. Bake the lasagna until golden brown and the apples are tender, 45 to 50 minutes. Remove from oven and let rest 10 minutes before slicing to serve.

[serves 8 to 10]

Fresh Apple Dessert Lasagna

Crisp, juicy apples fresh from the autumn trees are my favorite. This recipe takes on the traditional apple crisp as a unique way to incorporate lasagna noodles. The firmness and thick texture of the noodles lends a stability to the dish that makes presentation a cinch. Serve it with a scoop of your favorite vanilla ice cream, and you have a year-round winner.

¹/₄ cup melted butter

14 sheets phyllo pastry dough

Sugar

FOR LEMON CREAM:

³/₄ cup fresh lemon juice

1 teaspoon unflavored gelatin

6 tablespoons unsalted butter

2 tablespoons plus 2 teaspoons
lemon peel, grated

3 large eggs

3 large egg yolks

³/₄ cup sugar

1 cup chilled whipping cream

FOR CANDIED CITRUS STRIPS
AND SLICES:

1 large grapefruit

2 oranges

2 lemons

1¹/₂ cups water

²/₃ cup sugar

¹/₈ teaspoon vanilla

1¹/₂ tablespoons light corn syrup

FOR SIMPLE WHIPPED CREAM:

1 pint whipping cream

2 tablespoons sugar

¹/₂ teaspoon vanilla

Preheat oven to 400°F. Coat a large baking sheet evenly with butter. Unroll the phyllo dough. Place one sheet on a clean, dry work surface and spread it with melted butter. Place another sheet on top, and spread it with butter. Repeat until you have a total of seven sheets layered with butter. Cut the sheets into eight equal squares, approximately 4 × 4 inches. Repeat the process with another set of phyllo sheets so that you have a total of sixteen 4 × 4-inch squares. (Phyllo dough will dry out very quickly if not kept covered. Moisten a dish towel or paper towel with water and use it to cover the phyllo dough between usage.) Dust the top layer of each piece with granulated sugar, place in oven, and bake for 20 minutes or until golden brown.

Place 1 tablespoon of lemon juice in small bowl, and sprinkle gelatin over it. Let it stand about 10 minutes. Stir the butter, lemon peel, and remaining lemon juice in a small saucepan over low heat until the butter melts. Whisk the eggs, yolks, and sugar in a medium-sized metal bowl to blend. Gradually whisk in the butter mixture. Set the bowl over a saucepan of simmering water (do not let the bottom of the bowl touch the water). Whisk constantly until the mixture is thick and the thermometer registers 140°F for 3 minutes (about 8 minutes total). Remove from the water. Add the gelatin mixture to the hot lemon curd, and whisk until the gelatin dissolves. Chill to room temperature, stirring often, about 30 minutes. Beat the cream in a large bowl until medium peaks form. Fold the whipped cream into the curd. Cover and chill at least 4 hours and up to 2 days.

[To prepare citrus strips]
With a vegetable peeler, remove the zest from the grapefruit, oranges, and lemons in long pieces. With a sharp knife, remove any white pith from the pieces. Add the strips of citrus zest to a three-quart saucepan half filled with cold water; and bring it to a boil. Simmer for 10 minutes, and drain in sieve. In a heavy saucepan bring the water, sugar, vanilla, and corn syrup to a boil, stirring until the sugar is dissolved. Add the strips and simmer gently over low heat until translucent and the syrup is thickened, 15 to 20 minutes. Cool the strips in the syrup. Keep the candied strips covered and chilled for up to 2 weeks.

[To make simple whipped cream]
Mix ingredients in a medium-sized metal bowl and beat until soft peaks form. Sugar and vanilla may be adjusted to taste.

[To assemble]
Put one square of the phyllo on a serving plate. Spread it with whipped cream, the lemon cream, and finally the candied citrus strips. Top with phyllo, repeating twice, ending with a final layer of phyllo dough. Garnish the top of each lasagna with a dollop of whipped cream and candied citrus strips.

[serves 4]

Citrus Napoleon

Nothing says fancy like a layered dessert. In a rush? Substitute lemon pudding or canned lemon curd for lemon cream and store-bought whipped cream for homemade.

Preheat oven to 400°F. In a small saucepan, combine sugar, water, lemon juice, and cinnamon sticks. Bring to a boil, and reduce to a simmer for about 25 to 30 minutes until a thick syrup is achieved. Add honey and continue to cook for an additional 10 minutes. Remove from heat and allow to cool while assembling pastry.

Brush the bottom and sides of a 9 × 13-inch pan with melted butter. Phyllo dough will dry out easily. Have a damp towel available to keep dough covered and moist between usage.

Begin layering by placing six or seven sheets of phyllo pastry into the pan, brushing each thoroughly with butter before adding another sheet. Top the seventh phyllo sheet with ground nuts. Top the nut layer with two additional phyllo sheets, brushing each thoroughly with butter before adding another. Repeat the layering with nuts after every two sheets of phyllo; repeat until five or six layers of nuts have been used, brushing each layer with butter.

Top with the remaining seven or eight sheets of phyllo, buttering each one individually. Using a very sharp knife, measure the Baklava and cut it into diamond-shaped pieces. Do not cut all the way through the pastry, only halfway through it.

Brush the top with butter. Place in preheated oven. Reduce the temperature immediately to 375°F, and bake for 10 to 12 minutes. Lower the oven to 350°F and bake for an additional 30 to 40 minutes or until golden brown. Remove from the oven and cool for 10 minutes. Pour cool syrup over hot Baklava. Let set for several hours before cutting pastry, so syrup will drain through to the bottom.

Let it set overnight before serving. Do not cover airtight.

FOR SYRUP:

3 cups sugar

2 cups water

Juice from half of a fresh lemon

2 cinnamon sticks

3 tablespoons honey

1 pound phyllo pastry

1 pound butter, clarified

8 ounces pecans, ground

8 ounces walnuts, ground

[makes about 3 dozen diamond-shaped pieces]

Traditional Baklava

It seemed my Mom labored for hours over the many layers of phyllo, butter, and nuts in this dish, but the end result was always worth it. Today, I realize it doesn't take much time at all to make such a rich dessert.

A variation on the classic, this tiramisu has the rich flavors of coffee and Marsala wine and the subtle texture of the ladyfingers. Layered with a creamy filling, your guests will be delighted at the flavors, and you will be delighted with the ease of preparing it.

[serves 6]

Classic Tiramisu

To make the syrup, in a bowl stir together 1 cup sugar, boiling water, coffee, and 1/4 cup rum until the sugar is dissolved. Set aside. For the filling, beat the egg yolks and confectioners' sugar together with an electric mixer until pale and thick. Slowly beat in 1 tablespoon of the liqueur and the Marsala. Add the mascarpone cheese, and beat until the mixture is thick and smooth. Add the egg whites, folding to incorporate. Soak the ladyfingers in the syrup. Drop three ladyfinger pieces in the bottom of each of six wine glasses. Spoon in half the mascarpone, and sprinkle with half the grated chocolate. Repeat the layers with the remaining soaked ladyfingers, mascarpone, and chocolate. Cover and chill glasses for at least 2 hours. Before serving, top with whipped cream and toasted hazelnuts.

FOR SYRUP:

1/2 cup sugar

1/2 cup boiling water

1/4 cup strong brewed coffee (espresso is best)

1/4 cup dark rum

FOR FILLING:

3 egg yolks, reserving egg whites

2 tablespoons confectioners' sugar

2 tablespoons orange-flavored liqueur

1 tablespoon sweet Marsala

1 (8-ounce) container mascarpone cheese

3 egg whites, beat until fluffy and stiff peaks form

TO ASSEMBLE:

12 ladyfingers, broken into thirds

2 (1-ounce) squares semisweet chocolate, grated

whipped cream

1/4 cup toasted, chopped hazelnuts

4 cups ripe strawberries, hulled and thinly sliced

1 cup light red wine, such as a Charbono or Chianti

1/2 cup plus 2 tablespoons sugar

1/4 cup finely chopped walnuts

1/4 cup finely chopped pecans

2 tablespoons cinnamon

2 tablespoons sugar

1/2 teaspoon nutmeg, freshly ground

10 sheets of phyllo pastry dough, thawed and kept moist

2 sticks of unsalted butter, clarified

8 large egg yolks

Finely grated zest of 1 orange

1/3 cup Moscato or other sparkling wine

Large bunch of mint

Make-Ahead Ideas

Make the strawberries well in advance to ensure proper maceration of the juices. The phyllo crisps can be made a few days ahead and kept sealed in an airtight container. The zabaglione should be made fresh before serving.

Preheat the oven to 375°F. In a medium-sized bowl, macerate the strawberries with the red wine and 2 tablespoons sugar for up to 2 hours, stirring from time to time to dissolve the sugar.

In a small bowl, combine the nuts and set aside. In another small bowl, combine the cinnamon, sugar, and nutmeg, and set aside.

On a large, clean, flat work surface, unwrap and unroll the phyllo dough, being careful not to tear it. Dampen a paper towel with water to have on hand to keep the unused phyllo dough moist. Whenever the stack of

phyllo dough is not being used, make sure to cover it with the dampened towel, because the dough will quickly dry out and become brittle and unusable. Using the clarified butter, coat a 9 × 13-inch sheet pan (preferably a Teflon-coated one) thoroughly. Working in stages, separate one sheet of phyllo from the package, and place it flat on the buttered sheet pan. Brush lightly but thoroughly with clarified butter. Sprinkle with a dusting of the spice mixture. Repeat this process with five sheets of phyllo, buttering thoroughly between every sheet and sprinkling every sheet with spices. After the fifth layer of phyllo dough is coated with butter, sprinkle the nut mixture evenly over. Continue again with the layers of the remaining phyllo dough, buttering and dusting with spices after every one. Make sure that the last phyllo sheet is covered thoroughly with butter and

again dusted with spices. With a very sharp knife, gently score the phyllo dough so that it forms eight even squares. Only cut through the nut layer at this stage. Bake the phyllo sheets on the center rack until golden brown and crisp, about 20 minutes. Remove from the oven and let cool. Once they are cool, cut through to the bottom of the slices that you already created, ensuring that the phyllo is separated into eight equal parts. Set aside until assembling the dessert.

Put the egg yolks in a large, heatproof bowl, add the remaining 1/2 cup sugar, and whisk until light and fluffy. Bring a large pot of water to a boil over high heat. Whisk the orange zest and Moscato into the egg yolks. Put the bowl on top of the pot of boiling water, and whisk until the zabaglione is fluffy, stiff, and pale yellow, about 5 minutes.

[To assemble]
Place a phyllo square in the center of a dessert plate. Add a layer of strawberries, ensuring that the juice is running down onto the plate, then a scoop of zabaglione. Top with the remaining layer of phyllo, add another layer of strawberries, and top with a dollop of zabaglione. Garnish with a sprig of mint and serve.

[serves 8]

Spiced Phyllo with Strawberries and Zabaglione

Layers of crisp phyllo squares and sparkling sweet strawberries couple with creamy zabaglione in this elegant and simple dessert. Any fruit can be used to create dramatic layers in this dessert. When in season, strawberries are perfect with the champagne zabaglione.

Cook pasta noodles according to package directions, cool, and dry thoroughly. Combine the cinnamon and sugar in a small bowl. Once the pasta is dry, cut each sheet into thirds lengthwise.

Pour oil for frying into a heavy-bottomed saucepan, and heat on medium to high heat. Add pasta sheets in batches of two. They will appear to stick to the bottom of the pan. Do not attempt to scrape them loose. They should float to the top of the pot shortly after dropping in. If one persists in sticking to the pot, gently scrape or push it from underneath with a Teflon-coated spatula. Fry the pasta until golden, about $1^1/_2$ to 2 minutes on each side. Remove and place them on a paper towel. Sprinkle both sides of the pasta with the cinnamon-sugar mixture.

[For candied nuts]
Melt butter in a small skillet over medium heat. Add the chopped nuts and stir to coat with butter. Cook for about 5 minutes to toast, stirring constantly. Add sugar, brown sugar, cinnamon, nutmeg, and a pinch of salt. Combine and cook for an additional 3 minutes until the sugar is melted. Remove from heat and spread in a single layer on aluminum foil or waxed paper to cool.

[To make chocolate ganache]
Place the grated chocolate in a small bowl. In a small saucepan, heat the heavy cream just until bubbly around the edges, about 4 minutes. Pour the warmed heavy cream over the chocolate and stir until the chocolate melts. Add the butter and continue to stir until well combined. Set aside until assembly.

[For the crème anglaise]
In a small saucepan, scald the milk. Heat until the milk is just bubbling along the sides of the pan and steam is rising from the milk, about 4 minutes.

While the milk is heating, in a small mixing bowl, combine the eggs and sugar. Whisk them together until the mixture is smooth and pale yellow. Add about $1/_4$ cup of warm milk to the egg mixture, and whisk until combined. This is to temper the eggs to ensure that they don't scramble when added to the milk. Add the egg and sugar mixture to the milk, stirring constantly. Cook on low heat until the mixture has thickened slightly and coats the back of a metal spoon. (Do not allow it to boil, or the sauce will curdle.) Remove the pan from the heat and set aside.

[To assemble]
Paint each crispy noodle on one side with the chocolate. On a dessert plate, spoon crème anglaise in a circular fashion to "paint" the plate. Place one crispy noodle on the plate, chocolate-side up. Top with a scoop of softened vanilla ice cream. Place another crispy noodle chocolate-side up on top of the ice cream. Spoon additional crème anglaise on the top and sprinkle with candied nuts. Garnish with a mint leaf and dust plate with cocoa.

[serves 6]

Fried Pasta with Chocolate Ganache and Ice Cream

Fried pasta? You will love this dish. The crisp, cookie-like texture of the pasta, brushed with chocolate, is the perfect accompaniment to your favorite ice cream.

4 previously cooked pasta noodles, cut into thirds

1 tablespoon ground cinnamon

1 tablespoon sugar

canola or vegetable oil for frying

FOR CANDIED NUTS:

2 tablespoons unsalted butter

$1/8$ cup chopped pecans

$1/8$ cup chopped walnuts

1 teaspoon sugar

2 tablespoons brown sugar

$1/2$ teaspoon cinnamon

$1/4$ teaspoon nutmeg

salt

FOR CHOCOLATE GANACHE:

4 ounces semisweet chocolate, grated

$1/4$ cup heavy cream

1 tablespoon butter

FOR CRÈME ANGLAISE:

1 cup milk

3 egg yolks

$1/8$ cup sugar

$1/4$ cup warm milk

vanilla ice cream; mint leaves and cocoa for garnish

FOR THE PASTRY:

1 cup plus 1 tablespoon all-purpose flour

1/2 cup crumbled gingersnaps

1 teaspoon ground cinnamon

pinch of salt

8 tablespoons unsalted butter, at room temperature

2 large egg yolks, at room temperature

1/2 cup sugar

FOR THE PASTRY CREAM:

2 cups milk

6 large egg yolks, at room temperature

3/4 cup sugar

6 tablespoons all-purpose flour

generous pinch of salt

1 teaspoon vanilla extract

FOR THE FILLING:

1 1/2 cups best-quality, whole-milk ricotta

1/2 cup sugar

1 large egg yolk, at room temperature

zest of 2 lemons, minced

1/2 teaspoon lemon extract

zest of 1 orange, minced

In a wide mixing bowl, use a whisk to combine the flour, crumbled gingersnaps, cinnamon, and salt. Shape into a mound, forming a well in the center. Place the butter, egg yolks, and sugar in the well, mixing the contents of the well only to combine. (Using your fingers is generally the most effective way to do this.) Gradually work in the flour from the sides with your fingers (a fork can be effective as well). The mixture will become crumbly and feel like it is coming together; at this time use the heel of your hand to push it gently down and away from you, smearing it across the bowl. This will blend all the ingredients. When the dough holds together, pat it into a small disk, cover it, and let it stand for 30 minutes, allowing the gluten to relax.

Preheat the oven to 350°F. On a clean, dry work surface, roll the dough to ⅛ inch thick. The dough will be used to cover the bottom and sides of a 9-inch springform pan. Cut a disk out of the dough using the bottom of the pan as a guide. Fit the dough into the bottom of the pan. For the sides, simply cut the remainder of the dough into strips only so long that they are easy to handle. Wrap these strips around the sides of the pan, coming up about 2 inches from the bottom. Using your fingers, press all seams of the dough together, making sure that there is a consistent thickness throughout. Bake the dough, unlined and covered, until it is pale golden but not cooked through, about 15 minutes. Let it cool.

[For pastry cream]
Scald 1¾ cups milk in a medium-sized heavy saucepan over medium heat. Remove from the heat, cover, and let sit for 10 minutes.

In the work bowl of a food processor, whisk the egg yolks and sugar together until they are thick and pale yellow and a ribbon forms when you lift the whisk from the bowl, about 5 minutes. Add the flour and salt and continue to whisk until blended, then add the reserved ¼ cup of milk. Whisk the hot milk into the egg mixture, and add the vanilla. Pour the mixture back into the saucepan. Bring it to a boil for 2 minutes over medium-high heat, whisking constantly. Remove it from the heat and immediately transfer the pastry cream to a bowl to cool slightly.

[For the filling]
In the bowl of a food processor fitted with the blade attachment, mix the ricotta, sugar, egg yolk, lemon zest, lemon extract, and orange zest until blended. Add the cooled pastry cream, and mix until thoroughly combined. Pour the mixture over the prebaked crust.

Bake the torte in the center of the oven until the top is golden and a knife inserted into the center comes out clean, about 70 minutes. Remove the torte from the oven, and cool it on a wire rack for 10 minutes. Remove the sides of the pan and continue to cool it completely before serving.

[serves 12]

Citrus Ricotta Torte

While not a layered dessert, I thought it was fitting to add this recipe to the book because of its use of ricotta. The gingersnaps in the crust give a bite to the flavors, accentuating the citrus in the filling. Serve the cake chilled with an espresso.

chapter 7

A Few Key Recipes

Béchamel Sauce

Béchamel, or *besciamella,* is a basic staple of northern Italian cooking.

3¹/₂ cups whole milk

7 tablespoons unsalted butter

7 tablespoons all-purpose flour

salt

Scald the milk in a medium-sized saucepan (look for small bubbles forming around the edge) over low heat for about 4 minutes. Remove it from the heat but keep it warm. In another medium-sized saucepan, melt the butter over medium heat until completely melted. Whisk in the flour and let the mixture foam and cook, whisking occasionally, for 3 minutes or until it is a light tan color (you will notice a nutty aroma to the mixture). Slowly whisk in the hot milk and cook, whisking regularly, until the sauce thickens, about 5 minutes. If the milk has cooled, add it gradually in small portions, whisking between each addition to prevent lumps. If the sauce isn't thickening, increase the heat slightly and whisk constantly so as not to burn the sauce. Season the béchamel sauce with salt to taste and remove from the heat. Cool before using in lasagna dishes.

For added flavor, not necessarily suited for all dishes, stud one peeled medium onion with four whole cloves and place in the milk during the heating process. Remove the onion before adding the milk to the flour and butter mixture.

Bolognese Meat Sauce

This hearty meat sauce is probably the most traditional—with the exception of tomato sauce—in Italian cooking.

2 tablespoons olive oil

1 tablespoon butter

¹/₃ pound ground beef

¹/₃ pound ground pork

¹/₃ pound ground veal

3 ounces prosciutto, chopped finely

1 large onion, chopped

1 medium carrot, peeled and chopped

2 stalks celery, cleaned and chopped

3 garlic cloves, minced

2 sprigs Italian parsley, minced

1 bay leaf, crumbled

¹/₂ teaspoon fresh rosemary, finely minced

1 cup beef stock or broth

1 medium ripe tomato, peeled, seeded, and chopped

¹/₂ pound fresh mushrooms, sliced

1 cup dry red wine

¹/₂ cup milk

¹/₄ teaspoon nutmeg

In a large stockpot, heat the olive oil and melt the butter. Brown the beef, pork, veal, and prosciutto. Add the onion, carrot, celery, garlic, parsley, bay leaf, and rosemary, and cook on medium heat for 10 minutes. Add the beef stock and tomato. Cook for 5 minutes. Add the mushrooms and cook for an additional 5 minutes. Increase the heat to medium-high, add the red wine, and cook for 2 minutes until the smell of wine subsides. Add milk and nutmeg, and reduce heat to a gentle simmer. Simmer uncovered for 1¹/₂ to 2 hours until thick and hearty, stirring occasionally.

4 red peppers

2 tablespoons extra-virgin olive oil or 1 (15-ounce) jar of roasted red peppers, drained

2 cups heavy cream

1/2 cup freshly grated Parmesan cheese

1/8 teaspoon salt

1/2 teaspoon black pepper

2 cloves garlic, minced

2 tablespoons fresh chopped basil leaves or 1 tablespoon dried

[yields approximately 3 cups]

Fire-Roasted Red Pepper Sauce

[Roasting the peppers]

Wash and dry the peppers thoroughly. On a large platter, coat the red peppers with 2 tablespoons of olive oil. On a hot grill, under the broiler of an electric oven or over an open flame on a gas stove top, roast the peppers until the skin is charred black, turning them occasionally to ensure even roasting. When completely charred, place the peppers in a brown paper bag, sealing it shut for about 5 minutes. This technique will make it easier to remove the burned skin. Remove the peppers from the bag and remove the black skin, revealing the velvety, vibrant red flesh. Cut the peppers in half and remove the stems, seeds, and inner white veins. Chop the peppers coarsely and set them aside.

[Preparing the sauce]

In a heavy, medium-sized saucepan, heat the heavy cream. Add the grated Parmesan cheese, salt, and pepper to the cream and continue to heat it, stirring occasionally, until the cheese is melted and the sauce thickens. In the bowl of a food processor, combine the roasted red peppers and garlic. Process the mixture until you have a thick purée. Add the pepper purée to the heavy cream mixture and combine. Heat through. Add the basil and stir. Remove from the heat and set aside until ready to use.

The sauce may be made ahead and stored in a refrigerated airtight container for up to three days. During fall months, red peppers are in ample supply, with great quality and good prices. Roast the peppers any time and freeze them for later use. Make plenty of Fire-Roasted Red Pepper Sauce, package it, and freeze it for up to three months.

Roasted red peppers are a tremendous addition to any dish. Their robust flavors and silky texture add such characteristic flavors. For this sauce, either home-roasted or jarred roasted red peppers are fine. But if time and patience permits, I suggest the home method over store-bought. You won't be sorry when the end product is served.

Lasagna

Tips on Roasting Red Peppers

I have found that the easiest way to roast red peppers is on a gas grill. Turn the grill on high and roast the peppers until the skin is charred black, turning them periodically to ensure even roasting. If a grill is not readily available, the next best way to roast them (but a bit more dangerous and tedious) is on the open flame of a gas stove. Just turn the burner on high. Use a carving fork to pierce the stem end of the pepper to hold it, and roast over the flame until the skin is charred black, turning it continuously to ensure even roasting. Be careful in selecting the fork to use. If the handle is heat resistant, then you are fine; if not or if you are not sure, use an oven mitt so as not to burn your hands. As always be careful of the open flame, too. Make sure there are no animals or children around. If you have an electric stove, try the broiling method, which works fine, but is just a bit more messy and smoky. Turn on the broiler and place the oiled peppers in a roasting pan on the middle rack of the oven. Let them broil, charring the skin black, turning them occasionally to ensure even roasting. While this method actually sounds like the easiest (which it probably is), it doesn't yield the same effect and robust flavor of an open flame, thus the name "fire-roasted." The smokiness of fire and the sweetness of the peppers is a perfect marriage.

[yields 4 cups]

Quick Tomato Sauce

Quick and powerful, this tomato sauce takes little prep time (you don't even chop the basil) and little cooking time. The trick is fresh basil. While many recipes can handle dried as a replacement for fresh, I do not recommend it in this case. This sauce is simply too good with the fresh basil.

2 (28-ounce) cans best-quality, peeled plum tomatoes with juice

4 cloves garlic, peeled and coarsely chopped

1 tablespoon coarse salt

1 tablespoon sugar

6 tablespoons extra-virgin olive oil

1 cup loosely packed fresh basil leaves

2 tablespoons tomato paste

1/4 teaspoon black pepper

2 teaspoons dried oregano

1/4 cup red wine

Place all the ingredients in a large saucepan. Bring to a boil, stirring and boiling for about 5 minutes, crushing the tomatoes with the back of a spoon while stirring. Reduce the heat and simmer for 20 minutes, stirring occasionally. Serve immediately or refrigerate for up to five days. The sauce may be made, chilled, and frozen in airtight containers for up to three months.

FOR THE PROCESSOR:

2 cups tightly packed fresh
basil leaves

$1/2$ cup pine nuts

4 garlic cloves, chopped finely
before putting in the processor

salt

$1/2$ cup extra-virgin olive oil

FOR COMPLETION BY HAND:

$1/2$ cup freshly grated Parmigiano-
Reggiano cheese

2 tablespoons Romano cheese,
freshly grated

3 tablespoons butter, softened
to room temperature

[yields 4 cups]

Basic Basil Pesto

Briefly soak and wash the basil in cold water, and gently pat it thoroughly dry with paper towels.

Place the basil, pine nuts, chopped garlic, and an ample pinch of salt in the processor bowl, and process for a few seconds. Add the olive oil, scrape the sides of the bowl, and continue to process the mixture until a uniform creamy consistency is achieved. Transfer the mixture to a bowl, and mix in the Parmigiano-Reggiano and Romano cheeses by hand. It is worth slight effort to do it by hand to obtain the notably superior texture it produces. When the cheese has been evenly amalgamated with the other ingredients, mix in the softened butter, distributing it uniformly into the sauce. When spooning the pesto over pasta, dilute it slightly with a tablespoon or two of the hot water in which the pasta was cooked.

A Note on Cheese

Classical pesto is made with the Pecorino cheese known as Fiore Sardo. It is a less harsh flavor than that of Romano. Romano, however, is readily available. With this recipe, the proportion of Romano to Parmigiano-Reggiano is less than what you will want to use if you can get Fiore Sardo. Use $1/2$ cup Fiore Sardo to 2 tablespoons of Parmigiano-Reggiano.

Freezing Pesto

Make the pesto in the food processor, freezing it without the cheese and butter. Add the cheese and butter when it is thawed, just before using. Pesto may be frozen in an airtight container for several months. Summer is the best time of year for the freshest basil. Make yourself several batches of pesto and freeze them for when fresh, good-quality basil is not available.

Basil pesto, with its vibrant green color and tremendous flavor, is another Italian staple. It is as rich in history as it is in taste. Italian culinary traditions suggest that there is no other way to make pesto but by the mortar and pestle method, yet the nearly effortless food processor method given here is a fine substitute.

The long cooking time of this sauce establishes intense, concentrated flavors. Use this in place of the quick sauce in any of the dishes in this book or to simply top spaghetti.

[yields 2 cups]

Slow-Simmered Tomato Sauce

1/2 cup olive oil

1 medium onion, finely chopped

1 large carrot, peeled and finely chopped

1/2 cup fresh mushrooms, sliced

4 garlic cloves, minced

1 1/2 pounds ripe tomatoes, peeled

3/4 cup dry white or red wine

1 tablespoon fresh oregano, minced

1 tablespoon fresh basil, minced

1/2 teaspoon fresh thyme, minced

2 teaspoons sugar

2 tablespoons freshly grated Parmesan cheese

salt and freshly ground black pepper to taste

In a small skillet, heat 4 tablespoons of the olive oil, and sauté the onion and carrot until translucent, about 8 minutes. Add the mushrooms and garlic, and continue to sauté until tender. Remove from the heat and set aside. Heat the remaining olive oil in a heavy, medium-sized saucepan, and add the tomatoes. Simmer over low heat, breaking up the tomatoes with a wooden spoon, about 10 minutes. Add the onion, mushrooms, wine, garlic, oregano, basil, thyme, sugar, and cheese, cover, and simmer very gently for 2 1/2 to 3 hours. Season with salt and pepper.

Making Fresh Pasta Dough

Making fresh pasta dough is simple. There are some basic techniques to consider when making the dough, but nothing that relies on any amount of culinary expertise. I have included two methods for making the fresh dough: by hand and by food processor.

Now, I would be remiss in not saying that the "by hand" method is the classically preferred way to make truly great fresh pasta dough. The gradual process of hand-kneading the dough, coupled with the warmth from your hands, creates a far superior texture to the dough than a machine can do. However, in the interest of time and appropriate counter space in today's kitchens, the food processor method results in a great dough as well.

Fresh Pasta—By Hand Method

The amount of the flour is an approximate measurement due to the variable moisture in eggs, as well as the variation in humidity in your kitchen. You can adjust the amount before you begin to knead the dough.

2¼ cups all-purpose flour

3 large eggs, at room temperature

Pour the flour into a mound on a wooden or other smooth, warm work surface. (Stone or marble countertops are not a good surface for this because of their cold temperature). Using your hand, make a well in the center of the flour mound. Crack the eggs one at a time into the center of the well. Beat the eggs gently with a fork until the whites and yolks are evenly combined. Using the fork, begin to incorporate the flour gradually from the sides of the well into the eggs, stirring until the eggs are no longer runny. Be careful not to break the sides of the well because the eggs will run.

At this point, work quickly to incorporate the remainder of the flour with the egg. Using both hands, bring the remaining flour over the egg mixture, covering it completely. Work the dough with your hands until all the flour is combined with the eggs. This is where more flour may be needed. The dough should be moist, but not sticky. When it feels the right consistency, remove it from the work surface and wrap it up. Clean your work surface of all debris. Wash your hands to remove any egg or flour. Dry the work surface and your hands. Unwrap the dough and return it to the work surface. Begin kneading. Hold the dough with one hand, while folding it over with the other. Use the heel of your palm to push the dough down and away from you, continuing to fold it over. Rotate the dough a quarter turn during this two-part process of folding and pushing. Continue this kneading process until the dough is uniform and very smooth. Wrap it immediately in plastic wrap and let it rest for at least 20 minutes before rolling it out.

For Colored Pasta

Spinach pasta (green)

12 ounces fresh spinach, cleaned, or 7 ounces frozen spinach

[For fresh spinach]
In boiling, salted water, cook the spinach until tender, about 2 minutes. Remove it from the water, drain it, and squeeze it dry. Finely chop it before using.

[For frozen spinach]
Simply thaw and drain it, squeezing out any excess water. Finely chop it before using. Add the spinach to the beaten eggs, and incorporate it thoroughly before adding the flour. From this point, follow all the steps for making the fresh dough. More flour will probably be needed because of the added moisture from the spinach.

Tomato pasta (red)

3 tablespoons tomato paste

Add the tomato paste to the beaten eggs, and incorporate it thoroughly before adding the flour. From this point, follow all the steps for making the fresh dough. More flour may be needed; adjust this prior to the kneading step.

Food Processor Method

2½ cups all-purpose flour

½ cup cake flour

5 eggs, at room temperature

1 tablespoon extra-virgin olive oil

Place both flours in the bowl of a food processor fitted with the blade attachment. Pulse the flour to combine it. Beat the eggs together with the olive oil in a small bowl. With the processor running, add the egg-oil mixture to the flour. When the dough forms a ball, stop the processor. Remove the dough from the bowl, and place it on a clean, dry, warm work surface.

Begin to knead the dough, dusting it with a little flour to make it easier to handle. Follow the kneading techniques for the "by hand" method. Wrap the dough and let it rest for at least 20 minutes before rolling it out. For flavored or colored dough, add the spinach or tomato paste into the bowl with the egg and oil, using the same measurements as for the by-hand dough. The flour is an approximate measurement; more may need to be added. Adjust the flour prior to kneading.

Rolling the Dough

There are two techniques for rolling dough: by machine and by hand. Rolling by hand is done with a rolling pin. A long pin with no handles, similar to a wooden dowel, is preferred. While this technique is more labor-intensive and time-consuming, the result is a much more porous dough with a smooth texture, which will absorb sauces better.

[Rolling by hand]

Begin by unwrapping the dough and placing it on a clean, flat, warm work surface. Knead the dough for a couple of minutes to incorporate any moisture that may have gathered on top of the dough. Flatten the dough a little with your hands to make a round disk. Begin rolling with the pin from the middle of the disk, working outward to just before the edge of the disk. Rotate the dough ninety degrees and repeat the rolling. Continue this rolling until the dough is about ¼ inch thick. Repeat the process five times. This process is stretching the dough instead of rolling and flattening it. Continue to stretch it until it becomes transparent. Lay the dough on a kitchen towel in a warm, dry place to dry. When ready to use, simply cut the dough into rectangular noodles.

[Rolling by machine]

The pasta must be stretched and thinned out gradually. Pasta machines are equipped with an adjustable gauge that dictates the width between the rollers, allowing for gradual thinning.

Uncover the dough and knead to incorporate moisture that may have collected while resting. Cut the dough into six equal pieces. Working with one piece at a time and being sure to cover the unused pieces, knead the dough into a flat rectangle that will fit through the rolling machine. Set the rollers at the widest setting and begin passing the dough through. Pick up the dough as it comes through, being careful not to stretch it or pull it. Fold the dough in thirds. Turn it so that the folds are at the sides, and pass it through the machine again. Repeat this folding and rolling process three or four times until the dough is very smooth. Repeat with the other pieces of dough. Reduce the width of the machine by one notch. Pass all the pieces of dough through the roller once, laying them out on kitchen towels. Reduce the roller width another notch. Continue rolling all the pieces of dough on each width setting until they have each passed through the machine at the thinnest setting. Cut the pasta to desired size and set aside, covered, until ready to use.

Index

Acknowledgments

A cookbook is always a collaboration, a collection of thoughts, ideas, and contributions inspired by many family, friends, and colleagues. This book is no exception. For their many talents, skillful guidance, and creative graphic design, I wish to thank my editor Donna Raskin and art director Silke Braun, as well as Tim and Liz Prescott for their artful eye with food styling and Ron Manville, photographer and friend. A recipe doesn't become a published recipe without the discriminating and critical tastes of those chosen as recipe testers and tasters. Having a close circle of friends and family comes in very handy with this grueling task. I would like to thank Randy Mills, Steve and Erin Sears, Cliff and Kathy McGovern, Kerry and Brian Parent, and Richard Carbotti for their appreciation of good food and their unbridled approach to critiquing my food.

Thanks also to Tony Montefusco, the best friend and support a guy could ever wish for. Many thanks and much gratitude to Hans Stahl, for without his vision and confidence in me, this book would not be a reality. As you go along through life, there will always be those people you meet and befriend that will have some relevant impact on your present and future. To Martha Murphy, I thank you for your inspiration and friendship over the years. To my Camp Mystic friends and family—Dick and Tweety Eastland, Anne Eastland Spears, and Phillip and Jeanne Stacey— you gave me the opportunity and springboard from which I expanded my mind and talents in the kitchen; thank you. And of course a world of thanks goes to my family for their endless support and encouragement with whatever I do.

Lastly, thank you to all the readers who indulge in the pages of this book. Enjoy!